THINKING ABOUT EDUCATION SERIES
FOURTH EDITION
Jonas F. Soltis, *Editor*

The revised and expanded Fourth Edition of this series builds on the strengths of the previous editions. Written in a clear and concise style, these books speak directly to preservice and in-service teachers. Each offers useful interpretive categories and thought-provoking insights into daily practice in schools. Numerous case studies provide a needed bridge between theory and practice. Basic philosophical perspectives on teaching, learning, curriculum, ethics, and the relation of school to society are made readily accessible to the reader.

PERSPECTIVES ON LEARNING
D. C. Phillips and Jonas F. Soltis

THE ETHICS OF TEACHING
Kenneth A. Strike and Jonas F. Soltis

CURRICULUM AND AIMS
Decker F. Walker and Jonas F. Soltis

SCHOOL AND SOCIETY
Walter Feinberg and Jonas F. Soltis

APPROACHES TO TEACHING
Gary D Fenstermacher and Jonas F. Soltis

FOURTH EDITION

PERSPECTIVES on LEARNING

D.C. PHILLIPS
Stanford University

JONAS F. SOLTIS
Teachers College, Columbia University

Teachers College
Columbia University
New York and London

Published by Teachers College Press, 1234 Amsterdam Avenue, New York, NY 10027

Library of Congress Cataloging-in-Publication Data

Phillips, D. C. (Denis Charles), 1938—
    Perspectives on learning / D. C. Phillips, Jonas F. Soltis. — 4th ed.
            p.   cm. — (Thinking about education series)
        Includes bibliographical references and index.
        ISBN 0-8077-4447-6 (pbk. : alk. paper)
        1. Learning—Philosophy.   I. Soltis, Jonas F.   II. Title.   III. Series
    LB1060 .P48   2004
    370.15'23—DC21   2003065013
    98-20832

ISBN 0-8077-4447-6   (paper)

Printed on acid-free paper

Manufactured in the United States of America

11   10   09   08   07   06   05   8   7   6   5   4   3   2

Contents

Acknowledgments

As is the case with all books, this one owes much to those who have played a part in its production. Lee Shulman gave encouragement and agreed to use a draft of the first edition of the text in a course co-taught at Stanford with Denis Phillips. We are especially indebted to the students in that course for their constructive criticisms. Professor James Marshall of the University of Auckland carefully read and reacted to several draft chapters. Valerie Phillips and Frances Simon provided essential and much appreciated word-processing skills. For general research assistance that included copy editing, development of cases, and offering useful suggestions, we thank Karl Hostetler. For the second edition, we were guided by several thoughtful reviews of the earlier volume, and we were especially indebted to Kenneth Howe and Robert Floden. The substantial expansion of the discussion of social aspects of learning in the third edition owes much to what was learned from the "Symbolic Systems Seminar in Education" at Stanford over a period of about five years, and Rich Shavelson discussed some issues relevant to the revisions for the fourth edition. Finally, we thank the able and cooperative staff of TC Press for shepherding us through the four editions.

A Note to the Instructor

This book is designed to be used in the education of teachers. We did not write for "teachers in training" because we believe teachers should be *educated* rather than trained. We invite the users of the book to think with us as colleagues about the complexities of human learning.

The book is organized so that it can be used in a number of ways to suit the purposes and style of the instructor. It can be used singularly as the primary text for a full course on its topic, as supplemental reading, or as a source for cases and dialogues to stimulate class discussions.

If this book is used as a text in a full course, a number of pedagogical options are available:

1. The first eight chapters can be treated as you would treat any text, and then the arguments and issues in chapter 9 can be used to provide materials for class discussions for the remainder of the term. From our experience, a case or a dialogue can easily produce a good discussion that lasts thirty or more minutes.
2. We have found that doing a chapter and then spending one or two sessions discussing the cases and related dialogues is a very effective way to mix the theoretical with the practical. At the end of each of the first eight chapters and in table 1 in chapter 9 we have offered suggestions for additional cases, dialogues, and issues to be discussed as you proceed.
3. To either of the above approaches could be added your own or class-invented dialogues, debates, and puzzles that apply theory to practice or raise issues of personal concern.

If you have not taught using the case method before, the following suggestions may be of some help:

1. It is important to establish a good group climate for discussion in which individuals feel free to express their views openly without fear of ridicule and also feel free to challenge the honest views of others with reasonable arguments and genuine alternatives.
2. Good group discussions are facilitated by asking students to read cases and sketch their answers to case problems before class so a discussion can start with some forethought and direction.
3. Pedagogically, as a discussion leader it is useful to summarize along the way, to help students see the ideas at issue, and to bring in relevant theoretical knowledge to guide discussions to some reasonable conclusion however firm or tentative.
4. And remember, students can learn worthwhile things even when their instructor is not talking.

We trust you will find this book to be a versatile pedagogical tool, useful in getting students not only to learn about learning theories but also to think with and about them as they make practical applications and raise basic issues.

PERSPECTIVES on LEARNING

Chapter 1

Introduction

This is a book about theories of learning. In it we want to get you to think about learning—how it happens, and what it is. Obviously, as a teacher, your job is or will be to help others learn. You may already have some good ideas about learning—after all, you have been doing it yourself for some time. Or you may feel there is not much for you to think about regarding learning since modern learning theorists surely must know all there is to know about it by now. Perhaps all you need to do is read about their theories and heed what they say when you teach or design curricula. Unfortunately, that is not so easy to do. Theorists do not all agree about what learning is or how it happens. Psychologists, anthropologists, linguists, neurophysiologists, philosophers, and others are still trying to understand how the mind works and how people learn. Certainly, they have some good ideas that will help you think about learning, and we will deal with many of them in this book. But ultimately, it is you who will have to make the best sense you can of how to foster human learning in order to become a thoughtful and effective educator.

Learning

To get you into the right frame of mind to think about learning and to help you to see what this book is about, imagine that several of your friends were to contact you and ask a favor. One wants to learn to keep off junk food and seeks your advice and encouragement; the second is trying to learn Spanish vocabulary and asks you to act as tutor; the third has heard you debate in public, admires your skill, and wants your help in learning how to do it for herself; and the fourth friend is learning physics and is stuck on Einstein's theory, and he asks you to explain it to him. Being generous in nature, and also a very talented person, you agree to help all of them!

Clearly, in all four cases you would be assisting a person to learn. But it is also clear that the types of learning involved are quite different. In the first case you would be helping someone to break a habit; in the second you would be helping a person commit information to memory; in the third case you would be teaching your friend a new and complex skill; and your fourth friend needs to be taught something quite abstract. No doubt you would use different teaching strategies: the method you use to teach your friend to avoid junk food would not work with the learning of debating skills. And rote memorization, which works in the case of foreign words, is not likely to succeed with learning Einstein's theory. Your friend could memorize it, certainly, but this will not necessarily enable him to understand or apply it intelligently, and that presumably is what he is after.

The Teacher's Responsibility

How would you go about selecting a suitable teaching strategy in each case? How would you know that it was suitable? If one of your friends failed to learn, would you blame yourself for selecting a poor method? Teachers face these issues all the time, but with added complexity thrown in. They are not usually helping one person at a time, but are trying to promote learning in a class of perhaps thirty or more students. What teaching method would you use if all four of your friends turned up at one time? Furthermore, you are safe in assuming that your friends want to learn the things they have sought your help with, but this is not always a safe assumption to make in a classroom. Promotion of learning is not unidimensional—the importance of *motivating* students to learn cannot be emphasized enough; also important is catering for students who have different learning abilities and who cover the work at different rates, deciding what content to teach, maintaining discipline, and socializing students to become functioning members of society—all these are grist to the teacher's mill. Thus, anything you learn will have to be balanced against these other things; a teacher is constantly making difficult "judgement calls."

This book does not cover all the complexities of a teacher's life in the classroom—it is a book about theories of learning. In it we can only hope to stimulate you to think about learning, about the forms it takes, and about what you, as a teacher, might do to promote it in students. We cannot make you a good teacher. You have to do that for yourself. But thinking seriously about theories of learning should help.

The Variety of Theories

At this point you may have become aware of the suspicious fact that we have been using a key word in the plural: "theories" of learning. Why is there more than one theory in this area? There are several answers. In the first place, as we have already illustrated, there is more than one type of learning. It is not clear whether a theory that explains how habits are formed, or how facts are memorized, will also explain how a learner comes to understand a complex and abstract piece of science. (In the field of medicine, the "germ theory of disease" does not explain genetic defects—different types of phenomena require different explanations.) Of course, some researchers are trying to develop a single comprehensive learning theory; indeed, scientists in many fields are driven to integrate knowledge in this way, for if they are successful the results give a great deal of intellectual satisfaction and solve a number of diverse problems. But so far, in the field of learning, no such attempt has been a resounding success. Indeed, some theorists believe the mind is "modular," composed of a number of differently functioning systems that have been cobbled together in the course of evolution.

To help you see what we mean, consider some of the things you have learned in your life so far—and then think about how you learned them. For instance, most of us have learned directly from experience without instruction, study, or practice that ice is cold, flames are hot, water is wet, and knives can cut. However, when we learned the alphabet and how to count to ten, almost certainly we all required a little initial supervised instruction and needed to do some sing-song practicing. But it would be hard to think of learning to play chess or to drive a car without undergoing sustained instruction and without focusing one's mental efforts on the tasks embodied in the mastery of such things.

What do these examples suggest? First, there seem to be different sorts of learning, some simple and some complex, some involving the acquisition of knowledge and others involving the mastery of skills. Second, while some things can be learned without a teacher, there are many situations in which the help of a teacher is vital for many learners.

There is a possibility that different theories of learning have resulted from various investigators approaching the phenomenon of learning from different directions and armed with different initial "hunches." You may recall the old Indian folk tale about the blind men who were given an elephant to examine. The man who felt the tail got quite a different impression of the beast than the man who felt one of the legs, while the man who started with the trunk reached yet another startling conclusion. So it is in all scientific enquiries—the initial ideas or hypotheses the investigator forms may color his or her later conclusions.

Consider the following possibilities: If one were to focus on how a child learns that flames are hot and take this to be a typical case of learning, a particular (and probably narrow) experiential learning theory most likely would result. But such a theory probably would be different from one that would result from starting with a different case— say, how a child learns to count to ten. Neither of these theories, however, would be likely to be formulated by someone who had selected as a typical case of learning more complicated things like how people learn to drive a car or how high school students learn history. Thus, a psychologist or educational researcher who starts with the insight that humans are part-and-parcel of the animal kingdom may try to explain human learning in the same way that animal learning is explained (say, the learning processes in pigeons or rats). On the other hand, a researcher who regards the human brain as a type of computer, differing from the popular brands largely in that it is made of protoplasm instead of silicon chips, may try to explain as much learning as possible in data-processing terms.

It would be a mistake to think that only researchers hold such divergent, rival views. Teachers, too, vary a great deal in the underlying images they have of the nature of their students. Some regard all members of their school classes as being potentially equal in ability to learn, while others regard the students as inherently quite different; some regard the school as having great power to shape the minds of the students, while others regard it as being marginally influential at best; some see the students as unwilling and rebellious, while others see them as eager to learn and inclined to behave if they are treated properly.

Whatever your view on these matters, as a professional charged with fostering the intellectual development of your students, you should be acquainted with the variety of theories that have been put forward. Your eyes will be opened to new possibilities, and to facets of your students that you might otherwise not notice. Just as travel broadens the mind, so does acquaintance with rival viewpoints. You should reflect on the various theories of learning, and think about the implications that they have for your work in the classroom. The following chapters should help you set out on this professional journey.

The Plan of the Book

We will start with a consideration of two classical theories of learning that may appear simple and a little strange to modern eyes. But we will try to show that Plato's "recollection" theory and Locke's "blank tablet" theory offer some interesting ways to think about learning and set some problems and issues with which modern theories are still trying to deal.

Then we will look at behaviorism, a theory of learning that dominated the field of psychology for a large part of this century. The behaviorist takes learning to be the result of actions of the environment on the learner. For instance, we learn that a lightning flash is soon followed by thunder and so we also may learn to cover our ears whenever we see lightning. Sometimes we find our environment and our actions in it to be rewarding and so we learn to repeat actions that generally result in something nice happening to us. People who are good at ping-pong and frequently win tend to play more often than those who lose every match. According to this behaviorist theory, we learn to act in acceptable ways by being praised when we do good things and by praise being withheld when we do not.

The behaviorist theory has been challenged by a number of other theories and we shall consider the major challengers in subsequent chapters. Gestalt theory views learning as a process involving the attempt to think things out and then having "it all come together" suddenly in the mind. Sometimes it is jokingly referred to as the "Aha!" or "Got it!" theory of learning or, more seriously, the "insight" theory. It is like poring over your class notes before an exam and finally coming to see how the ideas dealt with relate to one another. To explain this mental phenomenon, the Gestalt psychologists looked beyond behavior and the environment, and they tried to throw light on learning by investigating tendencies of the mind to pattern and structure experience.

Beginning with a hunch about the importance of firsthand experience to learning, John Dewey developed a "problem solving" theory of learning whose basic premise was that learning happens as a result of our "doing" and "experiencing" things in the world as we successfully solve real problems that are genuinely meaningful to us. School learning then, he argued, must be based on meaningful student experiences and genuine student problem solving. He believed that textbook problems most often were not real problems to students and that school learning should be an experientially active, not a passive, affair.

Taking a biological approach, Piaget viewed learning as an adaptive function of an organism. By means of learning, an organism develops "schemes" for dealing with and understanding its environment. For Piaget, learning is the individual's construction and modification of structures for dealing successfully with the world. He also claimed that there are stages of intellectual development that all human beings pass through as they learn certain universal schemes for structuring the world (like the concepts of number, cause, time, and space) and as they learn certain aspects of logical reasoning. Piaget's ideas have inspired many subsequent theorists of learning, including the so-called radical constructivists.

A defect in many of the preceding theories is that they consider learning to be an *individual* phenomenon—the learner is depicted as a lone inquirer. In fact, of course, learners are embedded in a social network; teachers, parents, siblings, and peers, not to mention characters on TV and in films, all influence what each of us will learn. Chapter 6 discusses some basic ideas related to this theme of the social dimension of learning from Dewey, Vygotsky, and Bandura down to the advocates of "situated learning" and participation in communities of practice. Chapter 7 returns to the notion of "structure," this time with regard to the subject-matter to be learned. Since subjects are organized bodies of knowledge, it might help learners if they could see or construct for themselves the basic outline or structure of the subject they are studying. Dewey, Bruner, Schwab, and Hirst offer some insights into this process.

Finally, we shall look at an emerging theory of learning that comes out of our contemporary technological revolution in computing and artificial intelligence. This approach to learning theory has been called various things but perhaps the best catch-all term for it is the "cognitive science" approach. As we think about learning from this point of view we will have to consider to what extent computers are modeled on human minds and to what extent we can understand minds and learning by treating them as "computerlike." There maybe as many puzzles as there are answers and insights offered by this emerging view, but we know that it is one that has stimulated much contemporary thinking about learning and is sure to be of import to educators in the future.

The last chapter in this book, chapter 9, is somewhat different from the others. It is one we hope you will refer to and use as you go through the book itself because it is designed to stimulate further thought about the theories, problems, and issues raised in the book. We call this last chapter "Arguments and Issues." In it there are eighteen vignettes—concrete cases in the form of dialogues, disputes, arguments, and debates—that raise interesting and important issues about learning, and bring theory closer to practice. Whether you refer to some of the cases in chapter 9 as you go along, or save them for consideration at the end, we are sure you will find that class discussions of these examples will force even deeper thinking about learning and educating. For those who wish to sample some cases relevant to this first chapter before going on to chapter 2, we recommend "The Relation of Learning Theory to Teaching" and "Different Kinds of Learning?" in chapter 9. The book ends with an annotated bibliography of sources that will take you beyond our introductory treatment of theories of learning and keep you thinking about them as you become a professional educator.

Chapter 2

Classical Theories

Interest in teaching and learning is not new; it probably antedates recorded history. The New Testament paints a picture of Jesus as a dedicated teacher, consistently using stories and examples that would communicate his ideas in a memorable way to his audiences. A few years earlier, Rabbi Hillel also won fame as a teacher. Going back further, the ancient Greek philosopher Plato (428?–347 B.C.) expounded his ideas in lively dialogues, and his Academy was famous as a teaching institution. Plato, too, was concerned to use examples and stories that would make an impact. All this, of course, reflects the unsurprising insight that it is most effective to present material in a way that is both interesting and understandable to those who are to learn it.

But there is a problem here, and it is a tribute to Plato's genius that he was able to perceive it. How is it that a learner is able to understand something new? Consider a person who was absolutely and completely ignorant; how could this person understand, and learn, something that was totally incomprehensible? (Could a computer, with completely empty data banks and no internal program, acquire a piece of factual information without any prior preparation?) Plato had one of the characters in his dialogue *Meno* raise the issue in this way:

> I know, Meno, what you mean . . . you argue that a man cannot inquire either about that which he knows, or about that which he does not know; for if he knows, he has no need to inquire; and if not, he cannot; for he does not know the very subject about which he is to inquire.[1]

This problem, in one form or another, continues to plague researchers to the present day.

One answer that occurs after a little reflection is that learning depends upon the student having some prior knowledge or experience. A child who has not yet learned a language, and a computer that has not yet been programmed, cannot have anything "explained" to them. People listening to Plato or Hillel or Jesus would not be able to learn if they did not have enough experience to comprehend the parable being presented. A student who does not know that light has a velocity, and who does not have some understanding of the concepts of mass and energy, could not learn Einstein's equation (at least in the sense of understanding it and its implications).

Further reflection shows that, as it stands, this solution is no solution at all—at best it pushes the problem one stage back. For where did this previous knowledge come from? How was it learned? Presumably it was able to be learned because something prior to it was known. But, in turn, how was this learned? Here we are in the grip of an infinite regress—an uncomfortable situation to be in. Learning is possible only if some prior things are known, and these prior things could have been learned only if something prior to them had been learned, and so on!

Plato's Theory of Learning

The specifics of Plato's own solution to this problem seem rather fanciful to the modern reader, but the principle he adopted to escape from the infinite regress is one that is still in use: knowledge is innate, it is in place in the mind at birth. At the end of his famous work, *The Republic*, Plato included a myth describing the adventures of a young soldier Er who appeared to have been slain in battle, but who revived nearly two weeks later and was able to describe what had happened to his soul during the time he seemed to be dead. Er, together with the souls of those who actually had died, was able to gaze on the realm of everlasting reality, and thus come to learn the truth. Er also witnessed how souls picked new lives, and he saw that just before they were reborn the souls camped overnight on the banks of the Forgetful River. They were forced to drink from the river, where some drank more than their fair portion; by the middle of the night all souls had forgotten all that they had seen in heaven, and then they were swept away to their new lives on earth. The strong implication is that those who drank too fully would not be able, in the new life, to remember anything about reality, and these individuals would remain ignorant. Those who had drunk only the minimum, however, could with great effort—and with the prompting of education on earth—recall the insights into reality their souls had received. These latter would be the people who, on earth, would be regarded as having learned. In other words, for Plato learning was a process of recalling what the soul had already seen and absorbed; his theory (if we can call it that) even explains why it is that some people can learn more, or can learn more readily, than others. For Plato, teaching is simply the helping of this remembering process.

In the other dialogue we have mentioned, *Meno*, there is a famous

passage in which a slaveboy—who has never had any geometry lessons—
is led by a series of questions to invent for himself a theorem related to that
of Pythagoras, which states that the square of the hypotenuse of a right tri-
angle is equal to the sum of the squares of the other two sides. The point is
the same as in "The Myth of Er"; the slaveboy apparently has learned
something of which he was previously totally ignorant, but in fact it would
be impossible for him to do so, and really what has happened is that he has
recalled something that was in his soul (or, if you would prefer, in his
mind) all the time. According to Plato, if one does not previously know
something, one cannot learn it now! In later chapters of this book we will
see how twentieth-century researchers face up to Plato's problem—their
solutions are no less wonderful.

There is another important facet to Plato's view of learning, one
which some—but not all—recent writers have explicitly opposed. In an
important respect Plato regarded learning as a rather passive process in
which impressions are made upon the receptive soul or mind. After all,
Er learned by observing the realities in heaven. Plato tells another story,
"The Simile of the Cave," about some prisoners chained in a cave so that
they can look only at the wall furthest away from the entrance. Outside
the cave people pass by, carrying various objects held high above their
heads, but the prisoners can only see the shadows of the objects on the
wall. What they learn in their world of the cave is about these shadows,
which they mistake for knowledge of reality. Only if they are released
and allowed to turn around will they come to see reality and acquire
(learn) real knowledge. Plato was pointing out that many people who
think they are knowledgeable actually are quite mistaken. They take
appearance to be reality.

According to this simile, then, teaching is the process of releasing
people from the chains of ignorance; but it is also clear that learning is
passive, it is a matter of "turning" and allowing the mind to see clearly.
In other places Plato spelled out more clearly what is involved here, and
it is obvious that he valued the place of abstract reasoning; the person
who had been trained to reason clearly (logically and mathematically)
would be more likely to escape from the cave of ignorance and see the
truth by using his mind. But nevertheless seeing the truth was a kind of
seeing. (And, of course, we still say "I see it" when we have learned
something!) These points emerge in the following portion of Plato's
dialogue:

> We must reject the conception of education professed by those who say
> that they can put into the mind knowledge that was not there before—
> rather as if they could put sight into blind eyes.
>   It is a claim that is certainly made.

But our argument indicates that this capacity is innate in each man's mind, and that the faculty by which he learns is like an eye which cannot be turned from darkness to light unless the whole body is turned; in the same way the mind as a whole must be turned away from the world of change until it can bear to look straight at reality. . . .. Isn't that so?

Yes.

Then this business of turning the mind round might be made a matter of professional skill, which would effect the conversion as easily and effectively as possible. It would not be concerned to implant sight, but to ensure that someone who had it already was turned in the right direction and looking the right way.[2]

Case One

To help you think about the points Plato is making, imagine this teacher-pupil interaction:

P: Mrs. Smith, I can't figure out the answer to this math puzzle.

T: Which one, Henry?

P: The one that says, If you know that there are six grapes and two plums for each person sitting at a table and that there is a total of twenty-four pieces of fruit on the table, then you should know how many people are seated at the table . . . but I don't.

T: Sure you do. Think a minute. Could there be only one person?

P: No.

T: Why?

P: Because one person would get only six grapes plus two plums and that's eight pieces of fruit and there are more than that.

T: How many more?

P: Sixteen.

T: And if each person gets eight pieces, how many more people could there be?

P: Two! So there must be three people seated at the table!

T: See, I told you that you knew the answer. You just needed to get yourself in a position to see it.

Did the teacher tell or explain anything to the pupil? Did the teacher teach? Did the pupil learn something? What? Do you think this is an example of Plato's theory of learning? Why or why not? If you think about this case, and perhaps discuss it with others, we think you will see why Plato's myths and similes have stimulated the imagination of his readers for more than two thousand years.

Nevertheless, it is clear that the general answer Plato gave to the question "how is learning possible?" is not acceptable. If people can learn only if they have previous knowledge, then it is no solution to say that the soul acquired this previous knowledge sometime earlier by means of a process of observation. For how could the soul learn by observing unless it already knew something? (Imagine a computer wired to a TV camera—a set-up found in modern robots; the camera may "observe" the surroundings but unless the computer is programmed no information will be stored.) It is apparent that we are still in the grip of the infinite regress: Where did the original knowledge (or program) come from?

The Lockean Atomistic Model

A major attempt to answer this question was made nearly two thousand years after Plato. At the end of the seventeenth century the British philosopher John Locke (1632–1704) developed a theory of learning that was to profoundly influence the early development of modern psychology, as well as shape educational practice down to the present day. Locke shared some of Plato's assumptions but disagreed with him about others. Locke could not accept that knowledge was innate; in his view the infant came into the world with a mind that was completely devoid of content—it was like an "empty cabinet," a "blank tablet," or a "tabula rasa." On the other hand, Locke seems to have realized that *something* had to be present for the child to be able to learn.

Modern technology gives us an advantage that Locke did not have; there is a familiar and simple example that now can be used to illustrate the principles he had in mind. These days just about all of us have purchased a hand-held electronic calculator. It comes from the factory nicely packaged; when it is turned on it lights up but nothing else happens, for it has no contents in its memory. It is exactly analogous to Locke's newborn baby—it is a "blank slate." But lying dormant within the calculator are various powers or abilities or capacities to perform operations. The device lies ready to perform multiplications and additions, calculate percentages and square roots, commit numbers to memory, and so on. These powers or capacities have been wired-in by the manufacturers.

Similarly, Locke realized that the human infant is born with certain biologically preformed abilities, but these lie dormant. He was, of course, thinking about these matters long before the theory of evolution was developed, and he had no way to explain how the human species had come to acquire the various capacities and systems that it possesses. But just as the body was born with certain potentialities, so it was—for Locke—with the mind:

> In this faculty of repeating and joining together its ideas, the mind has greater power in varying and multiplying the objects of its thoughts. . . . it can, by its own power, put together those ideas it has, and make new complex ones.[3]

The mental powers or faculties that allow learning to take place, then, are "wired in"—they are part of the biological equipment of the human species. But these powers require ideas to work upon; they require some mental content. How does Locke account for the acquisition of these initial ideas? Again the analogy of the calculator is helpful. In order to use the device we must punch in some basic data via the keyboard; we may feed in, for example, $3 + 5 = $___. Only when some numbers are put "inside" the calculator will its powers come into operation. And these numbers come from the calculator's outside environment. So it is with humans. Locke's words are famous:

> Let us then suppose the mind to be, as we say, white paper void of all characters, without any ideas. How comes it to be furnished? Whence comes it by that vast store which the busy and boundless fancy of man has painted on it with an almost endless variety? Whence has it all the materials of reason and knowledge? To this I answer, in one word, from EXPERIENCE. In that all our knowledge is founded; and from that it ultimately derives itself.[4]

Locke's account of learning, then, is as follows: The newborn baby knows nothing, but it immediately starts to have experience of its environment via its senses. It sees shapes and colors, it hears things, it tastes and touches and smells. The resulting simple ideas (as Locke calls them) are retained because the mind has the power of memory. Gradually the child will use his or her powers of combination, abstraction, and so on, to build up complex ideas. The child also will experience certain "internal" phenomena, such as concentration, puzzlement, love, and rage, and from this there will be acquired certain other simple ideas that will be added to the rest. But no simple idea can be invented; if the child has not had the necessary experience, the simple idea will be missing, and this in turn will limit what can be produced in the way of complex ideas. A corollary of this is that all complex ideas can be traced back to the combination of a certain number of simple ideas.

It is easy for a modern reader to underestimate the power of Locke's simple model of learning. But its relevance for the work of the teacher is great. In the late nineteenth century several researchers realized that the early years of schooling were not as effective as they might be, because young children were assumed by teachers to have had more experience than actually was the case. Surveys in the United States, for example, showed that many of those starting school in urban centers had never seen common farm animals (some children thought that cows were only an inch or so large, because they had only seen drawings of them in picture books); many did not know more than a few colors, and others had never seen the sea. More recently, in the 1960s, we realized that children from low-income families lack a great many of the basic concepts that those coming from more affluent homes have acquired, and researchers hypothesized that this is one reason why many children quickly become low achievers in school. The U.S. federal government's "Operation Headstart" and the TV program "Sesame Street" were attempts to remedy this situation. Montessori schools, too, place a great deal of emphasis on the early sense experience of children, and they use a graded series of exercises with blocks of different colors, shapes, and textures.

All of these things are very much in the Lockean spirit; if children have not had a certain experience, then they will lack the related simple ideas, and as a result there may be deficiencies in the complex ideas they can build up (for some of the simple building blocks will be missing). One of the lasting contributions made by Locke is to alert us to the issue of prerequisites for learning: What experiences or simple ideas must a child have had in order to be able to go ahead and learn some new material? Teachers, in helping children to learn, do not think of this issue as often, perhaps, as they should. It is interesting to draw a contrast with computer programmers—in getting a computer to "learn" to perform some task, nothing can be taken for granted, and absolutely everything that the computer needs to "know" must be fed in. One slight omission, and the computer will not be able to perform in the desired manner. Maybe we should work on the principle that the same is true of human learners!

Case Two

Imagine the following teaching-learning episode. Ask yourself as you read it, does it illustrate Locke's theory? Can Plato's theory explain it?

T: Today, class, we are going to try to understand the theory of continental drift. Who can tell me what a continent is? Peter?

P: A continent is a very large land mass like North America or Africa.

T: And, of course, we all know what drift is, don't we? It's like putting a leaf in a stream and watching it move wherever the current pushes it. You've all seen that happen, haven't you?

Class: Yesss!

T: Now let's look at the map. If you could move North and South America across the Atlantic Ocean, how would those continents fit against the continents of Europe and Africa? Mary?

M: Quite well. I never thought of it that way but it's just like tearing a piece of cardboard and putting the torn edges back together again.

T: Do you think it's possible that long ago North and South America were connected to Europe and Africa in one large land mass which then broke off and drifted apart?

M: Looks possible, but how could something as heavy and solid as a continent drift across an ocean? Aren't the continents attached to the earth's crust?

T: Have you ever watched a pot of soup boil? The water bubbles up and pushes solid pieces in the soup away from the center toward the sides of the pot. Geologists believe that the inner core of the earth is hot molten matter that creates currents like those in a boiling pot. They have found a rift line in the middle of the Atlantic Ocean which is a thin part of the earth's crust and is made up of newer materials than the continents. So they hypothesize that the hot inner core of the earth leaks out at this "rift" and pushes the continents further and further away from each other since they first broke apart millions of years ago.

M: So, it's like the leaf drifting on the stream or pieces in a soup pot. The continents move because of the liquid movements below them. I see!

T: Class, any questions?

Class: Nooooo!

Before you read on you may find it interesting to go back to the "fruit on the table" case. Can Locke's theory of mental powers or faculties of reasoning explain what's happening to the pupil solving the math puzzle? Which theory, Plato's or Locke's, seems more satisfactory for interpreting the problem about fruit? Why? We shall revisit Locke's theory briefly in chapter 5 when we discuss modern "radical constructivists.")

A Critique

It would be a mistake, however, to think that the Lockean model of learning is perfect. One defect that Locke shares with Plato is the passive picture that is presented of the learner, especially during the early stages of the acquisition of knowledge. For Plato, the pupil was a spectator of reality; and for Locke, the mind was like an empty cabinet waiting to be filled. Very few things are as inert as a cabinet! As we will see in later chapters, more recent theorists of learning have emphasized the activity—both physical and mental—of the learner. Perhaps Locke had never closely observed a young baby, but certainly he missed the significance of the constant handling, sucking, and probing that goes on as the child learns about the world. To Locke, and probably Plato, experience is something that happens to a learner; but to more recent learning theorists, experience is something that a learner engages in, it is something that transpires as a result of the interaction between a learner and the surroundings. The philosopher and educationist John Dewey put it nicely; writing about American schools early in the twentieth century he said that

> those under instruction are too customarily looked upon as acquiring knowledge as theoretical spectators, minds which appropriate [gain] knowledge by direct energy of intellect. The very word *pupil* has almost come to mean one who is engaged not in having fruitful experiences but in absorbing knowledge directly.[5]

Dewey noted that the mind, the "organ" for acquiring knowledge, traditionally was conceived as being quite unrelated to "the physical organs of activity," and activity of the body was regarded as having nothing to do with learning. Indeed, activity was thought "to be an irrelevant and intruding physical factor." In contrast, Dewey stressed the link between learning and doing. He was a powerful critic of Plato and Locke, and he was a pioneer of "activity methods" in the classroom. We will examine his theory of learning in more detail later.

Another interesting aspect of Locke that has come under criticism is his atomism. Locke was a friend of the famous physicist Sir Isaac Newton and was much impressed by the method Newton had used—the method of breaking a physical system down (in theory) into its smallest parts, "atoms" or "corpuscles," and then studying what happened to these. In other words, Newton started with small particles and gradually pieced together a picture of what happened to a large object by combining what happened to the particles from which it was constructed. It will only take a moment of reflection for you to see that Locke was using the same method with the mind of the child. Complex thoughts or ideas were made up of numbers of simple ideas joined together in various ways. The simple ideas, the "mental atoms" or

"corpuscles," were the ingredients from which more complex mental entities, such as bodies of complex knowledge, were constructed.

It is a neat, fruitful, and captivating approach, which still can be used
to good effect in many areas. In the psychological domain where Locke
was using it, however, it runs into problems. For one thing, it is not at
all clear that experience comes to us in "atomic units" that get bundled
together into meaningful complexes by our minds. Consider the surroundings you are now in. There are an infinite number of things—
millions of specks of dust, shadows, patches of light, shades of color,
hundreds of objects both large and small, shapes and surfaces each
made up of millions of little areas, and so forth. There should be billions
of simple ideas forming in your mind as you look around you, but
obviously there are not. (In the words of William James, there should be a
"blooming buzzing Confusion.") There also are a number of well-
known optical illusions that are difficult for Locke's atomistic theory to
explain. For instance, the drawing of the candlestick that gradually
starts to look like two faces, or the two lines with arrow heads drawn on
them in such a way that one line looks longer than the other although
they are equal in size—if they are indeed equal then an atomist would
suppose that the idea we form about them would be that they were
equal.

In Locke's atomistic model, too, the simple ideas are combined together rather mechanically. For instance, simple ideas that occur together
would tend to be joined together by the mind. But could all learning pos-
sibly be that simple? Are meaningful complex ideas produced rather mechanically from simple ideas coming from experience? The work of the
teacher certainly would be easy if this were the case! Furthermore, all
pupils with normal intellectual "wiring," and with the necessary stock of
simple ideas (which only requires that they have had the requisite experience), would be able to learn everything. This would be an educational
heaven!

By way of illustration, we can refer to the myth that is believed by
some naive folk: It is sometimes thought that all that has to be done to
teach a child to read is teach him or her the alphabet. The reasoning
seems to be that words are simply mechanical groupings of the basic
units, namely, letters of the alphabet. But of course it is the words that
are meaningful—some would even say it is sentences—not the letters.
To understand the meaning of words and sentences you have to know a
lot more than the alphabet. The "doubting Thomas" can try the experiment of learning the Greek or Russian alphabet; it will not be much help
in trying to decipher the prose of Plato or Tolstoy. Change "letters of the
alphabet" into "simple ideas," and "words and sentences" into "com-

plex ideas," and you have here a nice criticism of Locke's atomistic model of learning!

Case Three

Suppose that we go along with Locke to the extent that we grant that humans are so "wired," so biologically constructed, that they have the capacity to interact with their environment and the capacity to remember and process information. How, then, can we make sense of the following case, which seems to be a straightforward example of learning but neither Plato's nor Locke's theory seems to be very helpful in explaining it. How would you explain it from your own experience if you were trying to invent a learning theory?

As a beginning teacher in the second grade at Mount Haven Elementary School, Judith Diaz found herself unable to control the children when they returned to the room after lunch and playing very active games on the playground. It seemed to take forever to quiet them down and no amount of her threatening, shouting, ignoring, or pleading seemed to hurry the process. She even tried bribing them with a dessert cookie if they would quiet down, but as soon as she gave out the cookies the spontaneous noise started again. As far as she was concerned, the first fifteen minutes of each afternoon session was lost to "simmering down."

Although she thought she had tried everything, one day she had an interesting experience. Having given up even trying to get order as the children took off their coats and hats and recounted their exciting playground experiences, she saw a small group at a far table sitting quietly examining an unusual object. She went over to them saying aloud, "How nice to find a quiet group!" When she saw that the "found object" was a gnarled piece of tree bark that looked rather like a frog she said, "Let me tell you a story about that wooden frog." Judith went on to tell an ingenious fairytale-like story about princesses, villains, magicians, kings, and a prince turned into a wooden frog. As she told the story, other children came quietly to listen while others quietly hung their coats with an ear cocked to listen too. In a few minutes (not fifteen!) things had settled down and the afternoon session was underway. That night Judith thought she ought to capitalize on this new technique that she had hit upon. She rummaged through her rock collection and found an interesting stone that looked like an unusual animal, and she made up a story about it. Next day, right after lunch she quickly quieted everybody down with the cookie promise, gave out the cookies, held up the rock, and began telling her story . . . but the children began talking to each other as usual and playing at hanging each other in the closet along with their coats!

Was yesterday an accident? Judith thought. Perhaps, but the more she thought about it, the more it seemed that somewhere in yesterday's experience was a way to help children learn to be quiet and to be ready to start class activities right away upon entering the classroom. The next day she looked around for any quiet person or quiet group and went over to Janie, Paul, and Hernando saying, "How nice and quiet you three are and so ready to start the afternoon. I've got a math game for you to play. Here, try this on your calculator and the first one to win the game gets to paint at the easel first." She then said, "Mary, Jack, and Sheena are quiet now. Come, I'll give you a math game to play, too." In short order, everyone was quiet and doing math. Judith tried the same thing the next day, remarking on and giving quiet students a choice of the first project of the day. In just a few days she found the children quickly quieting down as they came back from lunch and all she had to do once or twice a week was to say to them, "How nice to be able to start the afternoon so quickly and get everything in." On other days, they'd just start right in.

In this case, the students learned to be quiet, but does Plato's or Locke's theory explain how they learned that? How would you explain it?

To stimulate further thinking about this chapter we recommend "A Starting Place for Learning" in chapter 9.

Chapter 3

Behaviorism

The classical theories of learning discussed in the previous chapter were put forward before the field of psychology had separated off from philosophy as a discipline in its own right around the end of the nineteenth century. Plato and Locke were philosophers who had an interest in what we would now regard as psychological topics, but their method of investigating these topics was philosophical, not scientific. In fact, psychology only became a science—with the paraphernalia of experimentation, careful and systematic observation, measurement, and calculation—long after Locke's time. (The years around 1870 are often selected as marking the birth of modern experimental psychology.) The behaviorists worked after this watershed period; they were completely saturated with the scientific spirit—so much so that they may eventually have been misled. But their work has thrown a great deal of light on certain types of learning, and some of the principles they formulated are still useful ingredients in the armament of the teacher.

After publication of Darwin's theory of evolution in 1859, humans were seen as being "biologically continuous" with the animal kingdom. Humans may be different in many ways from the other species of animals, but at least so far as biological equipment is concerned (physiology, biochemistry, anatomy, and so forth) it became recognized that there were great similarities. In light of this, it seemed reasonable to expect that by studying biological processes in animals some insight would be gained into similar processes in humans. The great advances that have since taken place in the medical sciences have justified this approach. It was not long before researchers interested in psychological phenomena started working along the same lines. There was a spate of activity in the closing years of the nineteenth century onwards directed at how animals learn, the nature of drives and instincts, problem solving, and the like. Behaviorism developed out of this background.

Researchers working with animals seem to have a serious disadvantage that is not present for those psychologists who are studying humans. You can ask people to introspect and report what is happening in their minds—what they are thinking, what they are experiencing, what they remember, what they can see, how they feel—but there is not much point in asking a dog or cat or pigeon! Animal researchers, then, seem to lack this vital introspective source of data that is available to those who work on their fellow humans. It occurred to John B. Watson (1878–1958) that this supposed disadvantage was, in fact, very much an advantage.

The situation as Watson saw it in 1913 was that researchers working with humans had no reliable way of validating the introspective reports that people gave about what was happening in their minds. What is happening in your mind is accessible to one person only—you. But the essence of science is objectivity and replication; data have to be accessible to many researchers so that findings can be checked or reproduced by others. So Watson recommended that psychologists working with humans should use the same methods that animal researchers were using. The opening paragraph of his famous article in the *Psychological Review* in 1913, "Psychology as the Behaviorist Views It," was a vigorous call for a revolution, and it gave birth to behaviorism:

> Psychology as the behaviorist views it is a purely objective experimental branch of natural science. Its theoretical goal is the prediction and control of behavior. Introspection forms no essential part of its methods, nor is the scientific value of its data dependent upon the readiness with which they lend themselves to interpretation in terms of consciousness. The behaviorist, in his efforts to get a unitary scheme of animal response, recognizes no dividing line between man and brute.[1]

Every scientist must make assumptions in order to get his or her work started. One has to start somewhere. There has to be some basis from which the work will take off. Watson's paper is remarkable for the clarity and honesty with which it makes these assumptions or foundations explicit. But Watson's assumptions are tough ones. At first sight it looks extremely difficult to throw light on human learning, by not asking people about what they have learned, but by concentrating instead on their observable behavior. And it does not look too hopeful to try to understand how a person can learn something as complex as Einstein's theory, or debating techniques, by using principles and methods that were developed to study learning in pigeons and laboratory rats.

However, like Locke, the behaviorists assumed that humans were biologically "wired" or equipped so that they could interact with the environment, and profit from this interaction. But, unlike Locke and Plato, the behaviorists were not concerned about the origin of ideas or concepts. Plato's problem of how the acquisition of knowledge is possible unless something prior is known was not a problem for them—the behaviorists conceptualized matters differently. For the behaviorists, the issue was not how new *knowledge* is acquired, instead it was: How is new *behavior* acquired? In other words, to the behaviorists learning was a process of expanding the behavioral repertoire, not a matter of expanding the ideas in the learner's mind. (Mind, after all, was a subjective and nonpublicly observable entity, and thus had to be avoided by science.) In terms of a classroom example, the behaviorist is interested not in how a pupil understands and learns Einstein's theory, but in how a pupil can be led to behave in such a way that he or she can do certain things (such as get the correct answer to problems, perform experiments, write down certain equations when asked by a teacher, and so on).

How, then, do people learn, in the behaviorist's sense of acquiring new behaviors? What scientifically observable factors are at work? The answers to these questions come in two parts, for there are two traditions within behaviorism: on one hand there is classical conditioning or stimulus substitution behaviorism, and on the other, operant conditioning or response reinforcement behaviorism.

Classical Conditioning

Around the turn of the twentieth century the Russian physiologist Ivan Pavlov was studying the process of digestion in dogs, and by chance he discovered he was producing an interesting change in their behavior. (These days scientists have a technical name to make chance discoveries sound more impressive—they call it serendipity.) Pavlov noticed that whenever he fed the dogs, they started to produce saliva. It was produced even at the sight of food, just as you might "water at the mouth" when you see an ad for pizza or hamburgers on TV. Investigating further, he found that if he rang a bell at the same time that he fed the animals, after many repetitions just the sound (without the sight of the meal) led the dogs to salivate. The dogs had been conditioned.

It turns out that dogs, and indeed humans, have an inborn mechanism that stimulates the production of saliva when food is present (in popular language such a mechanism is often called a reflex action). The animal is "biologically wired" so that a certain stimulus (in this case, food) produces a specific response (salivation). Diagrammatically:

$$\text{stimulus (food)} \longrightarrow \text{response (salivation)}$$

or

$$S \longrightarrow R$$

What had happened in Pavlov's laboratory was that, in this natural reflex, a new stimulus (the bell) had become coupled with the natural stimulus (the food), and eventually it was able by itself to produce the original or natural response (the salivation). In other words, the new or conditioned stimulus replaced the natural stimulus. Diagrammatically:

1. natural stimulus (food) $\longrightarrow$ response (salivation)

2. natural stimulus (food)
       plus $\longrightarrow$ response (salivation)
   conditioned stimulus (bell)

and eventually,

3. conditioned stimulus (bell) $\longrightarrow$ response (salivation)

Watson was familiar with Pavlov's work, and he seized upon classical conditioning as the key mechanism underlying all human learning. Consider a homely example: How does a young child acquire the behavior of being difficult to put to bed in the evening? This is something the child has learned—but how? Who taught the child this undesirable way of behaving? The key is to find a natural reflex that produces the response we are considering (in this example, the difficult behavior at bedtime). Somehow the natural stimulus that produces this behavior has been replaced by a conditioned stimulus. Thus, a loud noise can produce fear and unsettled behavior—this is a natural or "wired in" reflex. Perhaps one night when the child was being put to bed, the parent slammed the door at the same time as putting out the light, and if the fright was severe enough the child might have become conditioned by this one event. In other words, the natural stimulus (the frightening noise) was coupled with the conditioned stimulus (the light being extinguished). The net result: whenever the light is turned off, the child becomes scared and unruly.

Watson saw these "built-in" behaviors everywhere (he sometimes called them built-in, rather than conditioned, behaviors because he wanted to stress for parents and teachers that they bore a great deal of responsibility for the things the child learned). He wrote:

The main point to emphasize is that practically every responding organ of the body can be conditioned; and that this conditioning takes place not only throughout adult life but can and does take place daily from the moment of birth (in all probability before birth). . . . All of us are shot through with stimulus substitutions of one kind or another which we know nothing about until the behaviorist tries us out and tells us about them.[2]

Undoubtedly Watson was right. Everytime a teacher shouts angrily at a class of pupils reading Shakespeare, a child might be adversely conditioned; the natural response to shouting and anger is to avoid whatever it was that the shouting was about. If the shouting or anger accompanied the reading of Shakespeare, then the Bard might in future be avoided like the plague. And if working under relaxed and quiet conditions naturally produces feelings of pleasure, and if mathematics is always done when these conditions prevail, then mathematics might become conditioned and produce feelings of pleasure. But to say that we are shot through with conditioned reflexes is not to say that our behavior consists *only* of conditioned reflexes. There are many cases of learning where accounts in terms of classical conditioning seem to be completely far-fetched. How can conditioned reflexes account, for example, for the learning of something as abstract as Einstein's theory, or even the learning of language?

All is not lost, for there is another mechanism to which the behaviorist can appeal.

Operant Conditioning

E. L. Thorndike (1874–1949) received his doctorate in 1898 for his study of the learning behavior of cats. Typically he would imprison a cat inside a box, which would have some simple release mechanism such as a chain or a lever that the cat could activate by touching. Upon release, the cat would be rewarded in some fashion—it would be given access to a piece of fish, for example. Thorndike recorded the time the cat took to escape over successive trials, and he graphed these to produce what is now known as a learning curve. It might be expected that on the first few trials the cat would be slow to escape, but soon it would "get the idea" and would learn to escape almost instantaneously. Instead, Thorndike found that there was a constant and gradual improvement; on each successive trial the cat would escape a little more rapidly, so that after many attempts (say, about a dozen) the cat would be getting out as soon as it was placed in the box.

As a result of this kind of work, Thorndike formulated several "laws of learning." His conception was that some nerve pathway had been established in the brain of the learning animal, so that when a particular stimulus was registered by the sense organs it became connected by this pathway to the organs that produced the response that had proven to be effective. His "law of exercise" was that the link between a given stimulus and response becomes stronger the more the pathway is activated; in other words, the more the behavior is practiced or exercised, the more strongly it will be established or "learned." His "law of effect" stated that if the response to a stimulus has a pleasing effect, then the probability would increase of the learner repeating that response when confronted with the same stimulus. (In terms of the cat, the first law means that the more times the cat practices escaping from the box, the better it will be able to do it; the second law means that if the response—the escaping—has pleasant consequences, such as access to fish, then if the cat is placed in the same stimulus situation again, it is more likely to repeat the rewarded response.) Diagrammatically, the "law of effect" can be depicted:

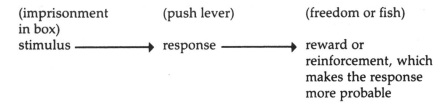

Thorndike was quite sure that these laws applied to humans as much as to simpler mammals. He wrote in 1913:

> These simple, semi-mechanical phenomena are the fundamentals of human learning also. They are, of course, much complicated in the more advanced states of human learning, such as the acquisition of skill with the violin, or of knowledge of the calculus, or of inventiveness in engineering. But it is impossible to understand the subtler and more planful learning of cultural men without clear ideas of the forces which make learning possible in its first form of directly connecting some gross bodily response with a situation immediately present to the senses.[3]

The mechanism for producing learning that Thorndike had hit upon in his "law of effect" was much more versatile than Pavlovian or classical conditioning. The latter is limited in that there has to be a preexisting reflex linking some natural stimulus and response; learning can only build upon this by "substituting" the conditioned stimulus for the natural one. But Thorndike's mechanism has no such limitation; any response to any stimulus can be conditioned simply by immediately reinforcing or rewarding it. The possibilities seem limitless, as was realized in the late 1930s by B. F. Skinner.

Case One

Before we look at Skinner's work, let us consider a simple case of one teacher giving some music instruction:

> Alright, play the chording as you practiced it. . . . You've lost the beat—keep time! OK, now try adding the right hand melody. Good. Wait, you've lost the timing again! Start again, please. OK . . . OK. Give it some feeling. . . . OK . . . OK . . . Good! Very good! Again. . . . Now you've got it! One more time to be sure it's in your fingers now. Play, don't think about it. Play. Excellent! Next week we'll do the next movement. Try the same technique, first do the chording then add the melody.

Can you use Thorndike's theory to explain this bit of learning? Does Locke's or Plato's theory add anything? Go back to the case at the end of the last chapter in which Judith finally got the class to learn to be quiet after lunch. Does operant conditioning explain this case? Is it only the students who were learning—acquiring a new behavior? Is Judith, herself, like the cat learning to get out of the puzzle box? Are the students being reinforced? But if so, why aren't they being reinforced by the cookies?

B. F. Skinner

Working with laboratory rats and pigeons, Skinner made some remarkable advances. He discovered, again by serendipity, that an action or response does not have to be rewarded or reinforced every time it occurs; he found that his rats learned very effectively if they were rewarded fairly frequently but randomly, but even better they then persisted with their newly learned behavior longer in the absence of reward. (An animal that has been rewarded for every action will soon stop performing if the rewards are cut off.) This is a common human experience; we all know that "a little praise goes a long way," and of course we find praise very rewarding. But we know also that we do not have to be rewarded for every right action we perform; an occasional pat on the back goes a long way. Teachers are well aware that praising a student for good work, or giving a gold star or some such reward, is very effective.

Skinner also found that he could "shape" the behavior of his laboratory animals in startling ways just by the judicious use of rewards. A famous demonstration, which he has done on film, is to teach pigeons to dance and to bowl a ball in a scaled-down ten-pin alley. Skinner takes a pigeon, and as soon as it makes the slightest move in the right direction it is rewarded. Then, when it eventually makes another move in the right direction, this is rewarded, and so it goes. In a matter of minutes Skinner can have the pigeon circling to the right or left. Quickly the dance is built up. He even has used this technique of "shaping behavior" via reinforcement to teach a pigeon to steer a guided missile!

He has applied these principles to human learning, for example, by way of his work with the teaching machine and the programmed text. These devices work on the principle that humans find that getting the right answer to a question is very rewarding. So in both the machine and the text, material to be learned is presented in small units, and the learner has to work through questions. If a correct answer is given, the learner receives immediate positive feedback and then moves on to the next item; if the answer is wrong, a "remedial" example or question is presented. As Skinner pointed out, the machine only presents material that the student is ready to learn (in the sense that the student got right all the steps that went before). The machine can give hints and prompts to help the student come up with the right answer, and "the machine, like the private tutor, reinforces the student for every correct response, using this immediate feedback not only to shape his behavior most efficiently but to maintain it in strength."[4]

Most people do not spend much time learning from teaching machines. But Skinner, no less than Thorndike, was confident that the mechanism of reinforcement of responses (operant behavior) was at work everywhere, in all types of learning. He wrote:

> While we are awake, we act upon the environment constantly, and many of the consequences of our actions are reinforcing. Through operant conditioning the environment builds the basic repertoire with which we keep our balance, walk, play games, handle instruments and tools, talk, write, sail a boat.[5]

To drive home the difference between Watson's behaviorism on one hand, and Thorndike's and Skinner's on the other, let us consider again the example of the child who is troublesome at bedtime. It will be recalled that Watson handled this case by locating some natural stimulus that produced the response (the unsettled behavior), and then he suggested that somehow the stimulus of turning off the light at bedtime had become substituted for this natural stimulus. Thorndike and Skinner have a different approach. They focus not on the stimulus that provokes the behavior, but instead they examine what happens to the behavior (or operant) after it has occurred. Thus, what happens to the child if he or she indulges in tantrums and so on at bedtime? Why, the parent comes in, turns on the light, and tries to comfort the child! In effect this is very rewarding—the child's response (the troublesomeness) becomes conditioned. No wonder it is repeated whenever the stimulus is the same, that is, at each bedtime. To change the behavior the parent has to extinguish this undesirable response, by ceasing to reward it; gradually, as was mentioned before, the now unrewarded behavior will die out.

Strengths and Weaknesses

Undoubtedly behaviorism has many positive features. For one thing, it is appealingly simple. It postulates that a single mechanism, conditioning, is responsible for producing learning, and furthermore, this mechanism operates throughout the whole animal kingdom. It is a mechanism that is easy for educators to master and put to good use; rewarding desirable behavior, and extinguishing (or even punishing) poor behavior, are techniques that all teachers can master (especially if they are rewarded for doing them). And there can be little doubt that these techniques are very effective—the animal experiments illustrate this, as do the variety of treatment programs that have been developed for human disorders such as autism, shyness, and antisocial behavior. The behaviorists, too, seem to bypass Plato's problem. Learning occurs not because there is something already present in the mind, but because, like other animals, we are "wired" so that any of our behavior that is reinforced is more likely to recur. Learning then, can be described simply as the acquisition of new behavior without reference to mental events.

Skinner's writings not only contain entertaining expositions of all these things; he is also an able philosopher, and gives a powerful defense of the underlying assumptions. He believes that it is quite unscientific for psychologists to make use of the notions of "mind" and "consciousness" in their theories and explanations. Psychology, as a science, must only make use of data that are objective and publicly accessible. Operant behavior, and the consequences that this behavior produces, are things that meet this criterion, but what is happening in the mind of the learner does not meet it. Skinner does not deny that something might be happening in the "inner experience" of the learner, but unless this somehow connects with the observable realm it cannot be dealt with by science. Thus, he writes:

> A purely private event would have no place in a study of behavior, or perhaps in any science; but events which are, for the moment at least, accessible only to the individual himself often occur as links in chains of otherwise public events and they must then be considered.[6]

All of this should force the educator to think seriously: Is learning best conceived as a change in behavior, or is something left out by this account? Are the events taking place in the mind of the learner of no relevance to the psychologist, and perhaps even more importantly, are they of no relevance to the work of the teacher? Just because operant conditioning undoubtedly has many useful applications in the classroom, does it mean that all cases of learning can be accounted for in these terms?

Has Plato's problem indeed been bypassed? Consider once more the learning of Einstein's theory. Maybe we can reinforce a learner after he or she correctly responds to a question about the theory, but it would be a tremendous fluke for the pupil to get it right in the first place unless the theory was understood, and to understand the theory wouldn't some prior things have to be known? The ancient Greek is not so easy to dispose of! Talking about behavior certainly hides the problem, but it does not dispose of it.

Three more of the difficulties that have arisen for behaviorism are worth mentioning here. First, Skinner's view of the nature of science is unnecessarily narrow. It is not true that scientists do not postulate unobservable entities or processes; in particle physics, for example, quarks with various quaint properties are supposed to exist, yet their connection to the actual data that physicists collect is extremely remote. Gravity is "invisible," but its effects are not. Second, Noam Chomsky has shown that a model such as Skinner's is not able, in principle, to account for the sort of phenomena that are met with in the field of linguistics. All of us, for example, can recognize the meaning of sentences and verbal constructions that we have never come across before. This is a particularly striking phenomenon in young children who are just learning their native language. So how could we have been reinforced to react to such sentences in some way, if we have never come across anything like them before? This cannot be how we learn our language. Finally, some experiments—of the sort that Skinner would admire—seem to indicate that something important is going on in the heads of learners, even laboratory rats. For instance, a rat might be taught to run a complex maze, by being positively reinforced by food when it reached the target; then, if some of the passageways of the maze are closed off, or if the maze is rotated through a large angle, the rat can still get to the target using some new passage—showing, apparently, that it had formed some sort of "mental map" of the maze by which it could guide itself!

The suggestion in this last example is that learners may form some sort of mental structure of their knowledge, and it is this that allows them to perform or to behave correctly. There has been a great deal of research done on this in recent years, which we will discuss in chapters 5, 7, and 8. First, however, we must look at another piece of the "jigsaw puzzle" about learning, a contribution that was made by Gestalt researchers who, throughout much of the twentieth century, were rivals and critics of the behaviorists.

Case Two

To give you a feeling for the Gestalt theory of learning and to set you thinking about whether the operant conditioning theory works as easily as Skinner claims in the interpretation of all kinds of learning, consider the following case:

> Joan had never before been interested in science. In fact, even though she was a bright student, she dreaded having to meet the middle school science requirements. But this term was different—really different. Ms. Cliff was an unusual teacher. Labs weren't done out of lab manuals. Instead, students arrived at the labs to find an array of items at each station and a "puzzle-problem" to deal with. This week the lab topic was electricity, which Ms. Cliff had talked about in class. On the lab table was a 6-volt battery that had a wire from each of its two terminals leading to two nails spaced about five inches apart and nailed into a board. One wire, on its way to its nail, was connected to a small flashlight bulb. The bulb was not lit. The problem-message for the lab was, "Try to make the bulb light using various materials available on the lab table to span the gap between the nails. Afterwards, write down what you think you learned from your experience." On the table

was a pencil, a pen, a spoon, a piece of paper, a beaker of distilled water, a salt shaker, a piece of curly telephone cord, a piece of string, and a 50-cent piece. There was a little note tucked under the half dollar saying it had better be there when the lab was over!

Joan thought she might as well try each object in the order it was found on the table. She placed the pencil so it touched both nail heads. Nothing happened. The same nonresult occurred with the pen, but the spoon made the bulb glow as soon as it touched both nail heads. The paper didn't work and the beaker was a bit of a problem. Holding it so the glass bottom touched the nails produced nothing, but how, Joan thought, could she test the water in it? She thought and thought and then in a flash she realized she could pick up the board, turn it over, and submerge the nail heads in the water. But nothing happened . . . maybe just a hint of a glow in the bulb, but not much. The salt shaker wouldn't reach the five inches, but Joan thought it might be interesting to shake some salt in the water to see if that made a difference. It did, the bulb glowed. She then poured a line of salt on the board to reach from one unit to the other. Nothing happened.

The piece of telephone cord was interesting. If she touched the outer plastic parts of the cord to the nails nothing happened, but if she touched the inner wire parts to the nails the bulb lit. The piece of string didn't work and Joan was left with the puzzle of how to test the half dollar. She thought and thought. There seemed to be no way to stretch it the five inches between the two nails and she knew it wouldn't dissolve in the water like the salt did. She just might not be able to test the half dollar. Already she suspected that metals were all good conductors of electricity and that if she could test the half dollar, it would work. But how to do it? Then she "saw" the way! She quickly unwound the wire from the nails and placed the tip of each wire on opposite edges of the half dollar. It worked.

Now she had to think about and write down what she had learned.

Imagine that you are Joan and have just had this experience. What did you learn? Which of the theories dealt with thus far help explain any of the learnings?

Before going on to the next chapter, you may want to consider the argument in "Learning and Behavior Change," chapter 9.

Chapter 4

Problem Solving, Insight, and Activity

The various theories of learning that have been discussed up to this point have had a number of features in common. First, they held that something is present in the learner at birth, something that allows learning to occur. They differed, of course, about what this "something" was: for Plato it was innate ideas and recollections of reality; for Locke it was inborn powers or faculties; and for the behaviorists it was some inborn physiology or "wiring" that allowed classical or operant conditioning to take place. Second, they all portrayed learning as a rather passive or mechanical process—the acquisition of knowledge, or in the behaviorists' case the acquisition of a new behavior, was more or less something that *happened to* a learner rather than being something that a learner *did* or *achieved*.

The theorists whom we shall consider in this chapter were strongly opposed to at least the second of these. For them, learning depended upon something being *done* by the learner. Indeed, one of them, John Dewey, wrote almost indignantly (and with Locke's model chiefly in mind):

> It would seem as if five minutes unprejudiced observation of the way an infant gains knowledge would have sufficed to overthrow the notion that he is passively engaged in receiving impressions. . . . For it would be seen that the infant reacts to stimuli by activities of handling, reaching, etc., in order to see what results follow.[1]

From this point of view the infant—and, indeed, every learner—is active, both mentally and physically, when engaged in learning.

The Gestalt Approach

Probably most of us were tricked, in childhood, by a friend who offered us a bet and then decided the winner by saying, "Heads I win, tails you lose!" If so, it was a classic "no-win" situation—our fate was sealed before the coin was tossed. One of the early Gestalt psychologists, Wolfgang Köhler (1887–1967), realized that much the same situation had occurred in psychology.

Köhler, a German, was stranded on the island of Tenerife by the outbreak of World War I, and thus he was able to put in several more years of work studying a group of chimpanzees in the scientific station there. Köhler was familiar with Thorndike's work, and he saw a serious defect in it. The way Thorndike had designed his experiments, he had eliminated all possibility of his cats being able to act intelligently. The cats were not given the information that would enable them to solve the problem that Thorndike had set them. He merely imprisoned them in a box, and waited to see if, by chance, they happened to trigger whatever escape mechanism he had built into the apparatus. (Imagine yourself suddenly taken and thrown into a cell. Could you reason your way out? Would you expect there to be a release mechanism? What if there was such a mechanism, but it was quite complex—would you discover it by accident? Would this be a promising setting for a researcher to do a study to find out if you were capable of learning?) Thorndike, then, had put his animals in a no-win situation: whether they were intelligent or not, they were in a situation where they could not effectively display whatever intelligence they did possess. And Thorndike's procedure virtually assured that learning would be found only to be something that *happened* to creatures!

Köhler decided to adopt a different and more revealing approach. He designed a series of problem situations for his chimpanzees, but in all cases every one of the elements that were needed for a solution was clearly visible to the animals. Thus, in one famous experiment with a chimp named Sultan, Köhler placed an "objective" (a banana) some distance outside the bars of the large chimp enclosure. But lying nearby inside the cage were two bamboo poles, each in itself too small to reach the banana. Sultan first tried to reach the objective through the bars using one stick, and then the other. He tried to push a nearby box through the bars, but quickly got it out of the way as useless. He even tried to put one pole through the bars, then push it to the objective using the second. After an hour Köhler abandoned the test, and left Sultan the two bamboo sticks to play with. A keeper who was watching reported what happened after Köhler had gone off:

> Sultan first of all squats indifferently on the box, which has been left standing a little back from the railings; then he gets up, picks up the two sticks, sits down again on the box and plays carelessly with them. While

doing this, it happens that he finds himself holding one rod in either hand in such a way that they lie in a straight line; he pushes the thinner one a little way into the opening of the thicker, jumps up and is already on the run towards the railings, to which he has up to now half turned his back, and begins to draw a banana towards him with the double stick.[2]

From this and similar experiments, Köhler drew the conclusion that learning takes place through an act of insight. The learner or problem solver must be familiar with the elements that constitute the problem and its solution, and the overall situation must be surveyable. The learner seems to mentally manipulate (and even, if necessary, physically manipulate) these meaningful elements until suddenly a "mental connection" is made between all of them. And as soon as the solution is "seen," it can successfully be put into action, as witnessed by Sultan's running to the bars of his cage the instant he realized that the two short sticks can be made into one that is sufficiently long.

Köhler, along with the other Gestalters—Wertheimer, Koffka, and Lewin, rejected the atomistic view of Locke that our minds receive simple ideas (like "yellowness," "hardness," and "coldness") that are later combined together into complex ideas. For the Gestalters, meaning is "built in" to the ideas we receive right at the start. The very word *Gestalt* means "organization" or "configuration," the point being that we experience the world in meaningful patterns or organized wholes. For the Gestalt psychologists, to dissect or analyze meaningful wholes into simple elements—as Locke's approach would have us do—is to distort.

How are we, then, able to be receptive to meaningful wholes in our surroundings? The key to this, for the Gestalters, had to lie in how our perceptual mechanisms—our eyes and ears and other senses—work (we actually *see* and *hear* wholes and patterns). In turn, the key to this also lies in the physics of how the electrical currents in our nerve circuits work. (Köhler was very much influenced by the field theory in physics developed by Max Planck, one of the great physicists of the early part of the twentieth century.) Once again, then, we see Plato's problem being answered in terms of something that is already present in the learner at birth—in this instance, it is the physics of the nervous system that allows insight, and hence learning, to occur.

The British philosopher, Bertrand Russell (1872–1970), was familiar with Köhler's work with chimps, and with the American work on animals in boxes and mazes. He wrote this provocative statement:

One may say broadly that all the animals that have been carefully observed have behaved so as to confirm the philosophy in which the observer believed before his observations began. Nay, more, they have all displayed the national characteristics of the observer. Animals studied by Americans rush about frantically, with an increasing display of hustle and pep, and at last achieve the desired result by chance. Animals observed by Germans sit still and think. . . . To the plain man, such as the present writer, this situation is discouraging.[3]

Discouraging perhaps, but certainly Gestalt psychologists stressed a point that is important in understanding human learning: We respond to meanings, we make intellectual connections. We learn Einstein's theory by achieving insight, by coming to "see" the link between certain ideas—not merely by reinforcement of our operant behavior. (Recall that Sultan's successful operant behavior, his manipulation of the sticks, was rewarded by his getting the banana, but the reward came *after* the behavior. How did he learn or "see" to put the sticks together in the first place before he was rewarded?)

Case One

Consider the following case as an illustration of Gestalt theory. Can it also be interpreted in operant conditioning terms?

Dick Johnson was a dedicated social studies teacher who was concerned about what his students gained from his courses, and was not solely interested in how they did on their final exams. However, the History of Western Civilization course always seemed to contain too much factual material and to be too disconnected, so he was concerned that his students were not really learning much history. There were so many dates, and so much time spent in describing the ancient, medieval, and modern periods that no matter how he tried, students never could "get it all together."

Last year, Dick had an idea. During the first week of the course he tried to show the students that the dates setting off the ancient from the medieval, and the medieval from the modern periods, were arbitrary and that historians didn't agree about them. He asked his students to think about the periods in their own histories (or personal biographies). The responses were great!

"I suppose I went through the stages of baby, kid, adolescent, young adult," said one.

"My stages were infant school, preschool, elementary, middle, and high school and, I guess, college," said a second student.

"What happens after college? Does your history stop?" asked Mr. Johnson.

Everybody laughed, but the teacher asked them to reflect on what comes after the modern period and on whether or not it someday will seem as ancient as Greek and Egyptian antiquity now seems for us.

Another student took a broader "personal history" perspective. "My great-grandfather and -mother came from Europe. He was a tailor and never went to school. My grandfather was a high-school graduate, and used his experience helping in the tailor shop when he became a salesman and eventually the owner of a men's clothing store. My father went to college and is an accountant in a large clothing merchandizing firm, and I'm going to try to become a lawyer—corporation law, I think. Dad's firm needs lots of them."

Dick Johnson turned to the analysis of these "self reports." The first "baby, kid . . ." history was put into periods and interpreted by using the familiar notions that describe life stages. The second history involving "schooling" was analyzed in terms of social-institutional stages or periods, and the third "great-grandfather" history was discussed in terms of occupational and educational descriptors. Mr. Johnson made it clear that during the term he wanted each student to read history, listen to his lectures, and try to find a way (that was sensible to them personally) in which to classify and interpret the history of western civilization as falling into periods—just as they had done with their own lives.

Dick Johnson gave pretty much the same assignments and lectures he had been using over the years. However, the results were startlingly different. On the final exam (which included only one item: Sketch the history of western civilization using your own periodic scheme), he got schemes such as the following:
Political orders: tribes, cities, city-states, empires, kingdoms, nation-states, nation alliance blocks, international government.
Economic developments: local economics, Mediterranean economy, European economy, colonization and world economy, international economy.
Dominant cultures and cultural forces: Babylonian, Egyptian, Greek, Roman, Catholic, Protestant, industrial, nuclear.
Students came up to him at the end of the course and remarked, "This is the first time I could remember any history without having to memorize it," "I never saw any connections in history before and now I do," and "History never made much sense before, now it does!"

It is not satisfactory to leave matters here, however. As it stands, "insight" is a mysterious, if not magical, thing. We need to find out more about what is going on "inside" the learner as he or she achieves it, and this will take us to the work of more recent researchers. But first there is the important contribution of John Dewey to consider.

The Inquiring Organism

John Dewey (1859–1952) is still regarded as America's most important philosopher, but he was also its leading educational theorist. In addition, he exerted an important influence upon psychology around the turn of the twentieth century. It was no accident that while he was at the University of Chicago (for about ten years spanning the old and new centuries) he was chairman of the Department of Philosophy, Psychology, and Education; perhaps never again have these three disciplines been so closely allied.

Dewey was born in the same year that Darwin's theory of evolution was published; at times this, too, seems more than a coincidence, for evolutionary biology became the major influence on Dewey's thought. Following the lead of the psychologist and philosopher William James, Dewey accepted that the human ability to think, and to learn, had evolved as had all the other capacities of living organisms. And capacities only evolve in a species if they contribute to its survival. (Think of the capacity to hibernate, in bears; the capacity to change color, in chameleons; or the capacity to use sound waves as a type of radar, in bats.) Thinking and learning, in Dewey's view, had evolved because they have a vital function—they enable humans to survive by escaping from danger, by foreseeing serious problems before they occur, by enabling foresight and planning and productive activity, and so forth. In other words, thinking and learning are "practical" capacities, in the exercise of which we actively interact with our surroundings:

> As activity becomes more complex, coordinating a greater number of factors in space and time, intelligence plays a more and more marked role, for it has a larger span of the future to forecast and plan for. The effect upon the theory of knowing is to displace the notion that it is the activity of a mere onlooker or spectator of the world. . . . If the living, experiencing being is an intimate participant in the activities of the world to which it belongs, then knowledge is a mode of participation, valuable in the degree in which it is effective.[4]

Dewey did not hesitate to draw out the educational implications of his evolutionary or functional view. In schools, too often students were treated in a manner that was quite contrary to the way in which thinking and learning functioned in the natural world. For in nature, thinking was stimulated by problems that the learner was vitally interested in solving; the learner was both physically and mentally active and alert and engaged. In schools, however, great effort was made by teachers to prevent physical activity—pupils were virtually imprisoned in their desks. Teachers set dry problems that may have been relevant for *them*, but which did not interest the pupils. Dewey vigorously advocated activity methods, and he argued that problems that were meaningful to the pupils must emerge from situations that fell within their interests and experiences. He did not mean, of course, that pupils should not be extended, that their intellectual horizons should not be stretched; it was a matter of where the teacher started, and how learning proceeded. In some respects, then, Dewey was preaching the same lesson as the Gestalters—Sultan thought, and learned, because the situation in which he found himself was meaningful to him, and it raised a problem that was of vital concern, namely, how to retrieve a banana!

Dewey did not deny that human learners can be *given* information by their teachers. But unless the learner had struggled personally with an issue, the information was likely to be committed to memory in a rather lifeless or mechanical way. He called this "static, cold-storage" knowledge, and he reasserted that unless the student had an opportunity to *use* the information in problem solving and action it was sterile: "information severed from thoughtful action is dead, a mind-crushing load."[5]

Dewey described the process of human problem solving, reflective thinking, and learning in many slightly different ways because he knew that intelligent thinking and learning is not just following some standard recipe. He believed that intelligence is creative and flexible—we learn from engaging ourselves in a variety of experiences in the world. However, in all of his descriptions, the following elements always appeared in some form: thinking always gets started when a person genuinely feels a problem arise. Then the mind actively jumps back and forth—struggling to find a clearer formulation of the problem, looking for suggestions for possible solutions, surveying elements in the problematic situation that might be relevant, drawing on prior knowledge in an attempt to better understand the situation. Then the mind begins forming a plan of action, a hypothesis about how best the problem might be solved. The hypothesis is then tested; if the problem is solved, then according to Dewey something has been learned. The problem solver has learned about the connection between his or her action and the consequences, almost in the same way that Sultan saw the connection between joining the sticks and being able to get objects that had been out of reach.

The Mind of the Learner

Let us grant, at least for the time being, that humans are "wired" or constructed (perhaps by evolution) so that they can profit from experience in ways that enable them to solve problems, achieve goals, and the like. And, let us grant as well that apart from chance, a problem can only be solved if both it and the ingredients of its solution are meaningful. What is happening in the mind of the learner as such a problem is solved?

This, of course, is the "sixty-four thousand dollar question." If it can be answered, we will have gone a long way toward discovering what a teacher can do to help a student learn. (Similarly, if Köhler had known what was happening in Sultan's mind, he would have been in a better position to help the chimp learn.) In fact, researchers in instructional psychology in the mid-1970s began to study the ways in which students think about their own thinking as they develop and use strategies for learning. They called this "metacognition." This line of work is promising, and may help to produce answers to this complex question.

We are moving to—or beyond—the limits of present-day computer technology, but our frequently called upon electronics analogy may still be of help. Imagine a mobile robot, equipped with a TV camera as a kind of eye, and controlled by a computer. (Some of these "creatures" do exist.) What would it have to "know" (that is, what data would it need to have stored) and what would it have to be able to do in order to learn from experience and to solve the problems it encountered in its ramblings? What would actually be happening inside its computer-brain as it achieved "insight" (that is, as it came up with a novel—not prewired—solution to a problem)? A tough series of questions, so no wonder they have not yet been fully answered! But, as will be seen, some exciting attempts have been made.

Before leaving the ideas dealt with in this and the previous chapter, you may wish to consider "The Scientific Status of Gestalt and Behaviorist Theories" and "Different Teaching-Learning Strategies," both in chapter 9.

Chapter 5

Piagetian Structures and Psychological Constructivism

Toward the end of the first decade of the twentieth century, Jean Piaget (1896–1980), a Swiss, was offered a full-time post as scientific curator of a museum collection of molluscs, on the basis of some papers he had published on the subject. He declined, on the grounds of age—he was still a secondary-school student! Thus began the career of the world's most eminent developmental psychologist, a man whose work has exerted extraordinary influence on contemporary views of the nature of learning.

His early biological training—he took his doctorate at the age of twenty-one for work on the evolution of the shellfish of Valais—indelibly stamped Piaget's approach to human learning. Like Dewey, he believed that the human capacity to think and to learn was an adaptive feature: its biological function was to aid the individual in dealing fruitfully with the surrounding environment. And, like Köhler, he carefully studied a small number of learners, setting ingenious little problems for them to solve, and making careful observations of their attempts. However, he did not study chimpanzees; he worked with young humans, particularly his own three children whom he studied intensively from the moment of their births. Furthermore, as a trained biologist he was comfortable with the notion that, in living organisms, important functions are carried out by biological structures. (Thus, the function of respiration is carried out by structures known as lungs or gills, the function of circulation of blood is carried out by a muscular structure, the heart, and so on.)

It is no surprise, then, that Piaget approached the function of thinking and learning in terms of the mental or cognitive structures that make it possible. Piaget seems to have regarded these structures as being quite real, although they are unobservable. It is quite scientific to study unobservables, providing one is careful about evidence and providing that any theories that are produced are testable by other scientists. (Recall that physicists often postulate unobservables.)

The Development of Cognitive Structures

Piaget was above all a developmentalist. He clearly recognized that children come into the world with minimal equipment to guide their behavior—merely a few inborn reflexes such as sucking and crying. Yet within a few years they are able to walk and talk, and deal with common everyday objects and situations. Within a few more years they become proficient problem solvers, and somewhere in their teens they are able to deal with quite abstract matters. What is happening during these formative years when children are learning so much?

In essence, Piaget believed that the developing child was busy constructing cognitive structures. At first the child had to learn to coordinate its physical movements—grasping, bringing objects to its mouth, and so on. Piaget spoke of the child constructing a schema for each of these complex activities; in terms of our well-worn computer and robot analogy, a schema is rather like a computer program. Thus, a mobile, computerized robot will have in its data banks various programs, or sets of directions, for moving its mechanical arm in various ways depending on the different situations it might encounter. The only difference, and of course it is a highly significant one, is that the Piagetian child *constructs* the programs personally (like learning to eat with a spoon), while present-day robots are *given* them. At any rate, at first the child is busy about this business, and Piaget distinguished this as his first developmental stage—the sensorimotor stage, lasting from birth to about the age of two. (A "developmental stage," of course, is another conception Piaget took over from biology; it is a commonplace that molluscs, insects, and so on pass through various stages during their life cycles.)

Like the learner depicted by Dewey, and even like Köhler's Sultan, the Piagetian child was described as very actively exploring its environment. As a result of handling, dismantling, and generally transforming its surroundings, the child gradually derived a set of concepts that were fruitful; at the same time the child started to "interiorize" its actions, that is, it started to build up a scheme or program of the actions it was performing upon its environment. Piaget called these latter conceptualizations "operations."

Now, the operations and other concepts being formed did not rest as a disconnected "lump" in the child's mind; they were interrelated or organized, and thus they formed a network, a cognitive structure. During the second developmental stage—the preoperational stage, from about ages two to seven—the child was still not able to conceptualize matters in the abstract, that is, to operate on them solely with the mind. The child had to have the concrete physical situation in front of it.

It will be recalled that in programming a computer, nothing can be taken for granted. Absolutely everything that the computer needs to have, either in its operating programs or in its data bank, has to be put there—the computer scientist needs to pay painstaking attention to detail. Similarly, if the computer was self-programming, everything it ended up "knowing" or being able to do would have had to be constructed from scratch. Now, there are many important things— things that are vital for dealing with the environment—that human adults take for granted, and most people do not realize must have been learned. Such things, for example, as the fact that physical objects have a permanent existence and do not cease to exist when they are out of sight, or, to take another example, the fact that the volume of a liquid does not alter when it is poured from one container into another of a different shape. Young children, Piaget discovered in a series of wonderfully striking experiments, do not know these things. Although "object permanence" is discovered quite early by the baby in its crib, conservation of volume, and the reversability of some operations (quantities that can be added together can be subtracted apart), and so on, are discovered relatively late. One of Piaget's most convincing demonstrations is worth describing: He took two identical balls of clay, and asked a child if one was bigger than the other. "No." Piaget then rolled one of the balls into a sausage shape and repeated the question. This time the child said the sausage was bigger. He then rolled it back into a ball shape, to be told it now had the same amount of clay as the other ball. Piaget found that only quite old children conserved volume and held that the sausage and the ball were still the same.

It is only during the third developmental stage—the concrete operation's stage, from about seven to eleven—that the child finally starts to conceptualize these things, and only after a great deal of actual physical experience with objects has accumulated. Piaget speaks of "logical structures" being constructed. At this stage, addition, subtraction, multiplication, and division can be done with numbers and not just with things.

Finally, its structures become close to those of the adult, and the young learner is able to solve problems in the abstract; conceptual reasoning has been mastered. This is the fourth stage, formal operations, from around the age of eleven to about fourteen or fifteen.

By way of summary, consider Piaget's words:

> Actually, in order to know objects, the subject must act upon them, and therefore transform them: he must displace, correct, combine, take part, and reassemble them. From the most elementary sensorimotor actions (such as pushing and pulling) to the most sophisticated intellectual operations, which are interiorized actions, carried out mentally (e.g., joining together, putting in order, putting into one-to-one correspondence), knowledge is constantly linked with actions or operations, that is, with *transformations*.[1]

Although this theory looks complex, there is a great deal of sense and order to it. Imagine our computerized robot again. If it were turned loose with only a minimal amount of direction, it would first have to "learn" to move effectively, and this would require it to produce a series of programs (action schemata). Then it would have to build up some information in its data banks about its surroundings—what the features were of the things it was bumping into, for example. Then, and only after it had acquired considerable experience, would it be able to formulate principles about how these things behave and what their properties were (object permanence, conservation of volume, and so forth). Finally, it would then be in a position to be able to predict beforehand (that is, "mentally") what might happen if it were to act in certain ways. The "logic" of this progression of stages seems fairly compelling—the robot could not make successful predictions about the behavior of things in its environment until after it had acquired an "understanding" of the properties of these things by operating on them, and in turn this would require that the robot have a stock of concepts in terms of which it could "think" about its environment.

So, then, there is a lot to be said for Piaget's view of the order in which knowledge is built up (although it should be noted in passing that criticisms of Piaget's work are mounting). But can anything more concrete be said about *how* structures are constructed?

The Principles of Construction

Biologists know that, in many instances, when one of the human body's delicately adjusted systems is thrown out of balance, say by some outside environmental influence, the affected system will respond so as to restore equilibrium. The human body has many feedback mechanisms that help to monitor and maintain constancy in this way. Consider body temperature: a rise of only a few degrees can have serious ill effects, and an increase of a few more can result in death. So, when faced with such a threat—let us suppose that the body is hot from extreme exertion—the body's systems respond by producing sweat, the evaporation of which is cooling, and also more blood is sent through the vessels near the skin in an effort to allow heat to escape. In this way the body accommodates to the presence of heat, and equilibrium is restored.

Piaget used a similar approach to explain how cognitive structures develop—he borrowed the biological notions of assimilation, accommodation, and equilibration. At any stage of his or her development, the young learner will be interacting with the environment, using whatever cognitive structures have been constructed up to that moment. If the experience is one that has been engaged in many times before, for example, being generally successful in judging the quantity of water in a glass using height as the key, the learner will be able to deal with it satisfactorily. The experience will be assimilated in terms of the present structures, and mental equilibrium will be preserved. Most likely, however, because the learner is still learning, his or her structures will not be able to completely handle some new experience (Piaget's ball and sausage of clay, or the tall-thin and short-wide containers of water). At some point there will be a loss of equilibrium, and some change (most likely an addition) will be made to a cognitive structure in an attempt to accommodate to the novel aspects of the experience. Thus the learner might acquire a new concept, or a new principle such as the principle of conservation of volume. In this way, little by little, in a cycle of attempted assimilation leading to accommodatory change and returning to equilibrium, more and more adequate cognitive structures will be built up:

> Intelligence, whose logical operations constitute a mobile and at the same time permanent equilibrium between the universe and thought, is an extension and a perfection of all adaptive processes. . . . Only intelligence, capable of all its detours and reversals by action and by thought, tends towards an all-embracing equilibrium by aiming at the assimilation of the whole of reality.[2]

Once again our trusty analogy is useful. Imagine our computerized robot let loose in a room that it has not yet completely conceptualized—it is still in the process of perfecting its programs and data banks. Suppose, then, the robot detects an object in front of it, and changes direction in order to avoid collision. So far, so good—the situation seems to have been assimilated to the robot's present knowledge. But suddenly, disaster! The robot hits the object it had attempted to avoid. Its internal equilibrium is upset, for the new direction was supposed to have prevented a collision. Accommodation of its data bank is called for, or perhaps of one of its programs. It might not, for example, have changed its direction of motion properly. So some change will be made (maybe its conception of the shape of the object is adjusted), equilibrium is restored, and the robot proceeds on its way until the next intellectual crisis. To an outside observer it may well look like a case of common trial-and-error learning.

We can imagine that in the long run, provided that the room is not altered, the robot will build up a perfect internal structure that never gets thrown out of equilibrium. The robot would then have intellectually mastered the problems associated with its movement around the room.

While this piece of science fiction helps to make Piaget's theory understandable on one level, it also serves to highlight a number of problems—problems the pursuit of which will push our understanding of learning still further along, until *we* reach equilibrium.

Case One

Before dealing with the critique, let us consider a case that seems to have some of Piaget's principles of learning embedded in it. As you read it, ask yourself to what extent Piaget's theory provides an adequate explanation. Can any of the other theories treated thus far be used to throw light on what was learned at Staple High?

Harry Strong, the math teacher and football coach at Staple High, took pride in both of his roles as a teacher. He not only taught basic skills in both areas, but helped students develop strategies for solving problems and dealing with difficulties. Team members and the math students liked Mr. Strong. He didn't yell at them when things went wrong; instead, he'd get them to think about what they were doing and how they might alter their strategies. Here are a couple of examples:

At half time last week, the team was losing to Central High. In previous years, when they had played Central, their opponents had run the ball mercilessly and Staple worked hard to contain this running attack. But this year Central took to the pass and caught Staple by surprise, quickly scoring three touchdowns. The defense was totally confused. In the locker room at half time, Harry Strong asked for an analysis, and the team agreed that they were poised primarily to stop the run. Now, however, it seemed they needed to change their strategy and to anticipate more passing. Mr. Strong made some changes in the defensive secondary, with the result that Central's passing did not hurt them as much in the second half. Even though they lost the game, they were able to come within three points and were proud of their effort. They had learned something in the process too.

One day last week Juan Valdez, Mr. Strong's best math student in geometry, brought in a problem he couldn't solve. Mr. Strong asked him how he was approaching the problem. Juan replied that he first tried to think of the axioms, postulates, and theorems that seemed relevant to a problem, then he would write them down and move them around into what intuitively seemed promising proof patterns. He showed Mr. Strong pages and pages of notes and scribbles trying different patterns, but none seemed to work for this particular problem. Juan felt that he had exhausted all the possibilities. "Why not try another approach," Mr. Strong counseled.

"Ever try a visual/figure drawing in the search for possible solutions?" he asked.

Juan hadn't, but it didn't take him long to follow this new lead. Mr. Strong put him to work at the blackboard, raised some helpful questions at the same time, and very quickly Juan found a solution to his problem and learned a new way to deal with geometric problems.

Some Critical Issues

In the first place, there are several mysteries concerning the mechanisms that, according to Piaget, lie behind the construction of structures. What does it mean to say that a cognitive structure has been put out of equilibrium? It is clear that a physical structure—say, a model made of building blocks, or a house of cards—can lose equilibrium, but a cognitive structure is *not* physical. It cannot topple over. This is just a misleading figure of speech. So, when Piaget asserts that a learner's cognitive structure changes because it is out of equilibrium, is he saying anything more than that it is changing? And if so, then he has not explained *why* change occurs. (It might be thought that Piaget could respond that the cognitive structure changes because it does not match up with reality, but this response would be like leaping out of the frying pan and into the fire. Who makes the judgment that the structure does not match? Are we implying that there is a little judge, an "homunculus," resting in the mind, that can see both reality and the cognitive structures and can compare them? Furthermore, Piaget—along with many other philosophers—seems to agree that each of us only sees "reality" through the medium of our cognitive structures, and so we cannot escape outside of these structures to see if they do correspond with reality!)

Similar problems beset the notion of accommodation. Hasn't Piaget again begged the question? When asked how it is we can learn a new concept, he replies it is because we make an accommodatory change. But what *is* an accommodation? Why, it is merely the adding of a new concept! He certainly has *named* the process, but has he explained it?

This leads to some other serious matters. Even if they were not subject to the criticisms above, the mechanisms postulated by Piaget are not powerful enough to account for the phenomena. For Piaget has insisted that *all children*, everywhere in the world, go through the same developmental sequence (although he also said that the ages at which children enter and leave the various stages will vary according to the society and the environment in which they are located). Now, when all members of a species pass through the same stages, the mechanism involved is a powerful one; in insects, for example, the stages of the life cycle are determined by genetic factors—that is why *all* insects pass from egg to larva to pupa to adult. But Piaget resisted saying the same thing about cognitive structures; they develop because of equilibration and the rest. Can such a mechanism be adequate?

To highlight the issue here, imagine several different robots let loose in a room. Is it at all certain that they would conceptualize it in identical ways? What if the room were very complex, and the objects in it behaved in intricate ways? It is not clear that all conceptualizations would be the same. Other researchers have felt the force of this problem and some have decided that at least the basic parts of cognitive structures must be predetermined by genetics. Linguist Noam Chomsky argues this way— the "deep structures" that govern acquisition of language by all humans are predetermined. Still others have held that social forces are at work steering the child's early attempts at learning (for example, parents, teachers, language, customs, the media), and this is why children develop along very similar paths. (All human societies, despite marked "surface" differences, work on basically similar lines, they argue. The Russians Luria and Vygotsky were prominent supporters of this general approach to human development as we will see in more detail shortly.) A common criticism of Piaget has been that he underemphasized the importance of the social environment; he did mention it, but generally it received little attention in most of his books.

If Piaget has not given a convincing account of how knowledge develops then he might not have escaped the force of Plato's problem. How *could* a computer, with nothing in it, develop something? How can a child, with no cognitive structures, start to develop them? There would be nothing there, at first, that could lose its equilibrium; there would be nothing there, at first, with which the world could be assimilated; and there would be nothing there, at first, that would require accommodations to be made. So, if there was nothing there, how could anything ever *get* there by the mechanisms that Piaget formulated?

Finally, there have been challenges made to some of the striking data that Piaget collected. His interviews with children, which yielded such interesting things as the "balls of clay" demonstration, were *clinical* interviews. They were often somewhat open-ended, and Piaget felt free to vary the procedure he was adopting in an interview, depending upon individual circumstances. Recently, researchers have suggested that other explanations are possible for the phenomena Piaget uncovered in this way; if very carefully controlled procedures are adopted, and rival hypotheses tested, they claim, the phenomena turn out differently.[3]

Guidelines for Educators

In the long run, it might not matter much if the details of Piaget's theory collapse under criticism. His work will still stand as a turning point—he showed the way to a new approach to understanding the developing learner. He has alerted us to a number of important things, even if he got the details wrong!

First, after Piaget, what educator who takes teaching seriously will ignore the fact that students may be developing through stages? Even more significantly, at some stages the students might not yet have developed the logical or conceptual equipment to be able to tackle certain types of problem—which is a different problem from their not having had the experience. The alert educator, then, will be concerned to select material that is appropriate to the developmental stage of the learner.

Second, after Piaget, who could ignore the role played by experience in education? A learner who has not encountered certain types of experience may also, and as a result, lack certain fundamental concepts. The learner might know the *word*, but this is not the same as having mastered the concept. (Every male parent has been embarrassed by the evidence that his offspring has learned the word "Daddy" but has not mastered the concept—thus, all men encountered, usually in the supermarket, are greeted with this title!)

Third, after Piaget, we should all be alert to the role played in learning not only by concepts but by principles such as conservation of volume, reversibility of logical operations, and object permanence as well as other mental categories treated by Piaget such as cause, time, space, and number.

Finally, after Piaget, only the insensitive teacher would be unaware that, in the course of learning, the student is not merely amassing concepts and operations and schema, but is *organizing* them internally in some way. Compare the ease of using a library that is logically laid out with one where the volumes have been thrown together haphazardly. A successful learner can readily retrieve what he or she has learned—a matter that will be pursued in the following discussion. Before continuing, you may want to give some thought to "Teaching, Learning, and Stages of Development" in chapter 9.

Constructivist Approaches to Learning After Piaget

Piaget's theory about how young learners construct their knowledge structures has been one of the inspirations behind at least some of the work done by members of the contemporary movement known as *constructivism* in education. Considered as a whole, this movement is very complex, and is made up of a number of (sometimes warring and quite incompatible) sects. One group, the so-called social constructivists, is concerned with how the public bodies of knowledge—the disciplines that form much of the content of the school curriculum that students struggle to learn, such as science, math, history, economics and so on—have been constructed by communities of inquirers over long periods of time. These scholars oppose the view that knowledge is built up by isolated individuals, and they stress that knowledge construction within the disciplines is a social activity. For an outline of this view, and a picture of the whole confusing constructivist scene, see the listing for Phillips in the "Annotated Bibliography" at the end of this book. We shall also touch on this social form of constructivism in the next chapter.

For our purposes in the present chapter, however, it is the *psychological constructivists* whose work is most relevant. These researchers focus upon how learning occurs in individuals and on how internal cognitive or memory or knowledge structures are built up or constructed. Some if not all of the figures we shall discuss in the next two chapters can be regarded as constructivists in this sense. But a particularly influential line of work that has been greatly inspired by Piaget is being carried out in the fields of science and mathematics education. One of the psychological constructivists working here, Ernst von Glasersfeld, is quite eclectic and seems to have been influenced by empiricist philosophers such as John Locke in addition to Piaget and the Continental philosopher Immanuel Kant. Von Glasersfeld refers to himself as a "radical constructivist."

In brief, von Glasersfeld argues that the individual learner is *not* the recipient of knowledge that is pressed onto his or her consciousness by some "external reality." In this regard he differs markedly from Locke and also from Plato. But, similarly to Locke, he seems to hold the view that each individual is only in "contact" with the impressions (or stimuli or experiences) that are received via the sense organs. Thus the task for the learner is to construct a body of knowledge on the basis of these sense impressions, knowledge that will help the individual to adapt to the environment in which he or she is situated. One of the controversial "twists" that von Glasersfeld gives to this basic story is that he asserts we have no grounds for believing in any form of "external reality"—each one of us seems to subjectively construct a functionally adequate set of beliefs, but these cannot be held to "objectively represent" whatever reality exists external to our cognitive apparatus! (Here von Glasersfeld seems indebted to Kant, who referred to this "external realm" as the realm of "things in themselves" or "noumena"—which are unknowable.)

Nor can we suppose, according to von Glasersfeld, that other individuals construct structures that in any way resemble our own; teachers cannot assume that the "understandings" of their students resemble their own. It might even follow, from this position, that each of us has no solid grounds for believing that other individuals exist—after all, *you* might merely be a "construction" that my mind has made![4] On the other hand, Piaget believed that the knowledge constructed by all individuals has the same structural features, and the reason we make the same or similar constructions is because we are dealing with the same reality.

Some of these complexities emerge in the following passage written by von Glasersfeld as part of the introduction to a collection of essays:

> The notion that knowledge is the result of a learner's activity rather than that of the passive reception of information or instruction, goes back to Socrates and is today embraced by all who call themselves "constructivists." However, the authors whose work is collected here, constitute the radical wing of the constructivist front. . . . This attitude is characterized by the deliberate redefinition of the concept of knowledge as an adaptive function. In simple words, this means that the results of our cognitive efforts have the purpose of helping us cope in the world of experience, rather than the traditional goal of furnishing an objective representation of a world as it might "exist" apart from us and our experience.[5]

What would a constructivist teacher be like? This is not a simple question to answer definitively, and in the literature there are hundreds of references to this topic. Furthermore, as von Glasersfeld stresses, radical constructivism does not entail that there is only one right way to teach, so it cannot

> produce a fixed teaching procedure. . . . As I have often said, constructivism cannot tell teachers new things to do, but it may suggest why certain attitudes and procedures are fruitless or counter-productive. . . .[6]

This point is well-taken, but nevertheless we think there are strong grounds for claiming that a good constructivist teacher will be indistinguishable from a good progressive educator who works according to the principles put forward by John Dewey. Students will be actively engaged with interesting and relevant problems; they will be able to discuss with each other and with the teacher; they will be active inquirers rather than passive; they will have adequate time to reflect; they will have opportunities to test or evaluate the knowledge that they have constructed; and they will reflect seriously about the constructions produced by other students and by the teacher.[7]

It is easy to see the similarities between Piaget and the radical constructivists. Among other things, they share a common concern with what is happening in the adaptive cognitive apparatus of each individual learner. As we shall see in the next chapter, however, there are strong intellectual currents in the contemporary world that move us in a more *social* direction.

Chapter 6

Social Aspects of Learning

Before pursuing the important notion of structure in more detail, a serious limitation—involving many of the theories that have been discussed up to this point—requires further comment. In varying degrees, the work of Plato, Locke, the behaviorists, the Gestalt theorists, Piaget, and von Glasersfeld all harbor this defect: *the learner is depicted as a lone investigator.* Certainly the learner may be actively interacting with the environment (in the depictions of Piaget, Kohler, and the behaviorists), or may be a passive recipient of stimulation or experience (according to Locke and Plato)—but what is missing from these accounts is detailed exploration of the fact that learners by necessity belong to social groups. Learners have parents, siblings, teachers, peers, and fellow learners, with whom they communicate and interact, and from whom they receive guidance and stimulation. Learners interact with adults who are generally more proficient than they are, they discuss their puzzlements and engage in activities with their friends (using the social medium of language), and they read books and magazines and watch television (the various forms of media are, after all, devices for communication produced within society). Any account of learning that gives short shrift to these diverse social factors to some degree must be deficient. (At this point the comparison with computers and hand-held calculators that has served us well—and to which we shall return in following chapters—reaches its breaking point. The analogy might be saved if we consider the role of the computer programmer, who in a sense acts in a manner similar to a teacher or a parent. But even so, we are only referring to a single person effecting learning, and our point here is that all of society and its media are teachers.)

The points made above barely scratch the surface of the topic of indebtedness of growing individuals to their social-cultural environment. Most forms of learning (certainly the sorts that are of professional relevance to us as educators), and most human communication, would not be possible without language; and language is a social medium (the philosopher Wittgenstein even has an argument to show that an absolutely private language is impossible—even a "secret code" is merely a translation of a natural language.) This is not to deny that animals (which cannot speak), and very young children at their pre-linguistic stages of development, are still able to learn by imitation or by behaviorist-style "shaping" of certain of their spontaneous behaviors; but the learning of history, literature, mathematics, science, aesthetics, and such things as the principles of morality, are all enterprises in which language plays a crucial role and thus, at base, are social enterprises.

Furthermore, the bodies of knowledge that have been built up in history or science, or the literary canon, and so forth, are all social products in the sense that researchers, writers, and philosophers have contributed to the construction of these bodies of knowledge over long periods of time, using such social processes as discussion, argument or debate, criticism, publication or public demonstration and dissemination, collaboration or teamwork, and adjudication or refereeing of disputes. It is worth reflecting on the fact that different societies existing in the present day, and societies in different historical periods of their development, each have or had particular bodies of knowledge—and also intellectual tools and techniques—that are or were regarded as important for learners in those societies to master. In other words, what educators attempt to pass on to learners in every society is socially determined! No wonder, then, that the social construction of knowledge—"social constructivism"—is currently a topic of great interest to philosophers, sociologists, and feminist theorists.

In present-day advanced societies there is a tendency for us to overlook the obvious facts mentioned above, because of the long-standing Western individualistic/liberal tradition that has been passed on to us as part of our own social heritage. We tend to think that in some historical or logical sense individuals came first, and then at some crucial stage in human history they decided to band together to form societies in order to gain mutual benefit. In other words, individuals *decided* to form societies—it was a rational choice. (Rousseau even wrote a book on "the social contract" that, he pretended, these rational ancestors of ours entered into when they formed early societies!) These days scholars regard all this as a fanciful myth; there *never* was a time when humans did not live in groups—we *are* social animals, who actually evolved within groups, and in all probability we developed from pre-human ancestors who also lived in groups. Thus living together, communicating and interacting, working cooperatively on tasks with other members of our social group, and so forth, are the historical *norm* for humans, not a late "add on." Our ancestors became rational *within* groups—it was not the case that they became rational and *then* formed groups. The ethnographer Clifford Geertz has made the interesting (and at first sight quite paradoxical) point that it is even within a social or cultural group that we become individuals; he wrote:

Becoming human is becoming individual, and we become individual under the guidance of cultural patterns, historically created systems of meaning in terms of which we give form, order, point, and direction to our lives. As culture shaped us as a single species—and is no doubt still shaping us—so too it shapes us as separate individuals.[1]

As we shall see in the following discussion, the philosopher and educationist John Dewey was well-aware of the social nature of learning; he even advocated adopting a social perspective on the whole educational enterprise:

> Education, in its broadest sense, is the means of this social continuity of life. Every one of the constituent elements of a social group, in a modern city as in a savage tribe, is born immature, helpless, without language, beliefs, ideas, or social standards. Each individual, each unit who is the carrier of the life-experience of his group, in time passes away. Yet the life of the group goes on. The primary ineluctable facts of the birth and death of each one of the constituent members in a social group determine the necessity of education.[2]

We must now return to the issue of how learning occurs in a social context. A good place to start is to return to the work of Piaget, who tended to give an individualistic rather than a social account: the Piagetian child is, in essence, a young researcher, busily exploring the environment and constructing schemata in solitary play. When the child faces a problem, he or she makes some accommodatory change to restore cognitive equilibrium. In much of his writing Piaget gives the impression that this is a solitary endeavor—the child seems to make such changes without help from anyone. Even when an adult is playing with an infant (as when the parent is hiding the baby's rattle under the blankets in the crib, or is rolling a ball of clay into a sausage shape), the *child* is the one who eventually discovers (or, perhaps more accurately, invents) an accommodatory change that will enable sense to be made of what is happening and that will restore equilibrium.

But is this what really happens in most cases? Don't most adults who interact with a child give it clues about what is happening when there is a puzzle? "Does this sausage of clay *really* have more in it than the clay ball? How can that be? I haven't put more clay in, have I?" This kind of remark is a direct hint to the child about what sort of accommodatory change is likely to pay off—it is a hint about the principle of conservation of matter. Granted, young children *do* spend much time in solitary play, but there is still a great deal of nurturing interaction with other human beings that Piaget seems to downplay. This deficiency is even more pronounced when we consider how people learn something on the order of Einstein's special theory of relativity. Most of us (with the possible exception of Einstein himself) learned this theory from a textbook, with a teacher or classmates peering over our shoulder or working with us, ready to offer advice and further explanation as we struggled with the difficult material. We did not learn about the theory by reinventing it for ourselves, or by accommodating entirely by ourselves when we were out of equilibrium. We were given, or sought out, social resources for learning it.

John Dewey

John Dewey, whom we met in a different context, was extremely sensitive to the social nature of learning. In a passage in an earlier chapter that Piaget would have done well to ponder, Dewey wrote—similarly to Geertz—that:

> As matter of fact every individual has grown up, and always must grow up, in a social medium. His responses grow intelligent, or gain meaning, simply because he lives and acts in a medium of accepted meanings and values. Through social intercourse, through sharing in the activities embodying beliefs, he gradually acquires a mind of his own. The conception of mind as a purely isolated possession of the self is at the very antipodes of the truth . . . the self is not a separate mind building up knowledge anew on its own account.[3]

Dewey stressed that the school was a *community*, but too often educators overlooked this by keeping students isolated at individual desks. This stifled both pupil activity and communication. In contrast, Dewey wanted schools to engage students in meaningful activities where they had to work with others on problems. Purposeful activity in social settings was the key to genuine learning in Dewey's view. (It is commonplace, even today, for students to be punished or chastised by teachers for talking with each other, even though in most situations in the adult world people learn by communicating with their fellow workers!)

The teacher's task in all this was to "provide the conditions that stimulate thinking" and to take a sympathetic attitude; the teacher had to participate in "a common or conjoint experience" with the learner.[4] Under no circumstances was just *telling* the student about a new idea very effective—the student would come to learn this new thing by rote, but would be unlikely to understand it or see its relevance and connection to other ideas. The best way to learn a new idea, according to Dewey, was by means of "normal communication with others"—the process of communication in which the learner was interacting with others in purposeful activities or investigations of common interest.[5] Modern researchers, such as education sociologist Elizabeth Cohen,[6] have paid a great deal of attention to the organization and management of productive groupwork in schools.

Case One

In his famous novel *Oliver Twist*, Charles Dickens described what happens when young Oliver, lost and destitute, is given refuge by the master pick-pocket and thief, Fagin, and his band of young criminals including "the artful Dodger" and Charlie Bates. Before the gang is sent out for each day's "work," Fagin "warms them up" with the following game, which also serves to train new members like Oliver:

> When the breakfast was cleared away, the merry old gentleman and the two boys played a very curious and uncommon game, which was performed in this way. The merry old gentleman, placing a snuff-box in one pocket of his trousers, a note-case in the other, and a watch in his waistcoat pocket, with a guard chain around his neck, and sticking a mock diamond pin in his shirt: buttoned his coat tight around him, and putting his spectacle-case and handkerchief in his pockets, trotted up and down the room with a stick, in imitation of the manner in which old gentlemen walk about the streets any hour in the day. Sometimes he stopped. . . . At such time he would look constantly around him, for fear of thieves, and would keep shaking all his pockets in turn, to see that he hadn't lost anything, in such a very funny and natural manner, that Oliver laughed till the tears ran down his face. All this time, the two boys followed him closely about, getting out of his sight, so nimbly, every time he turned round, that it was impossible to follow their motions. At last, the Dodger trod upon his toes, or ran upon his boot accidentally, while Charlie Bates stumbled up against him behind; and in that one moment they took from him, with the most extraordinary rapidity, snuff-box, note-case, watch-guard, chain, shirt-pin, pocket-hand-kerchief, —even the spectacle-case. If the old gentleman felt a hand in any one of his pockets, he cried out where it was; and then the game began all over again.[7]

What theories of learning are helpful in explaining the various things that are learned here? Why did the participants (including the onlookers) find this game so engaging? What is your opinion of Fagin as a teacher? Before continuing with the next section, you might consider the case "Individualized Instruction" in chapter 9.

Vygotsky and Others

Another writer who was well-aware of the social nature of learning was the Soviet psychologist Lev Vygotsky (1896–1934). An essay published posthumously in 1935 contained the following recognition of the flaw in the Piagetian approach:

In experimental investigations of the development of thinking in school children, it has been assumed that processes such as deduction and understanding,
evolution of notions about the world, interpretation of physical causality, and
mastery of logical forms of thought and abstract logic all occur by themselves,
without any influence from school learning. An example of such a theory [can
be seen in]Piaget's extremely complex and interesting theoretical principles.[8]

In contrast to Piaget, Vygotsky did not assign much importance to the
"stage" of development at which a child might be, for Piagetian stages
(and IQ, for that matter) were only a rather "static" indicator of what intellectual tasks a child could accomplish *on his or her own*. Vygotsky, aware
that learning takes place in social settings, was more interested in the learning *potential* that a child might have—what the child might accomplish
with the guidance of adults or older peers. He recognized that two children might be at the same Piagetian stage or have the same IQ, but that the
potentials for further development of each, when properly challenged or
stimulated, might be markedly different. He invented the notion of the
"zone of proximal [or potential] development" (now often referred to as
the "ZPD") to deal with such cases.

Vygotsky's ideas have been quite influential in his homeland, but only
relatively recently have become more widely known in the Western world.
The following is a brief account of how Russian psychologists of a few
years ago determined a student's zone of potential development:

> A typical testing session consists of the initial presentation of a test item exactly
> as it would occur in an American IQ test with the child being asked to solve the
> problem independently. If the child fails to reach the correct solution, the adult
> progressively adds clues for solution and assesses how much additional infor-
> mation the child needs in order to solve the problem. The child's initial perfor-
> mance, when asked to solve the test item independently, provides information
> comparable to that gained with standardized American IQ testing procedures.
> The degree of aid needed before a child reaches solution is taken as an indica-
> tion of the width of his potential zone . . . the level of competence he can reach
> with aid. In addition we gain information of the child's ability to profit from
> adult assistance, his speed of learning.[9]

This aspect of Vygotsky's work seems to be helpful to teachers, who as a
matter of educational strategy probably should not treat their students as if
they are frozen at some definite intellectual state, and thus as if they are in-
capable of further growth or development. On the contrary, schooling is
based on the assumption that students will learn when placed in groups or
other educational settings devised by expert teachers.

In further contrast to Piaget's self constructed schemas, Vygotsky stressed that much of what we learn we learn from others. Moreover, what is most important to learn from others are those "psychological tools" that human societies have invented to allow individuals to deal effectively with each other and the world.[10] Logics, symbolic transformation, concepts, forms of notation, signs, numbers—like the hammers and saws of carpenters—are the "tools" humans use to build a view of a world they inhabit together. When a learner acquired a new "psychological tool," new possibilities are opened up. Here are two examples: first, a young child's capacity to remember is greatly expanded when she learns to speak, and has acquired a vocabulary in which to formulate things to commit to memory. Second, it is impressive how many new types of problems, and how many situations, can be dealt with once a school-aged child has acquired some mastery of decimal notation (many problems that are almost impossible to solve using fractions become "child's play" when formulated this new way—even the relatively simple "fourteen and two-thirds multiplied by ten" becomes a push-over when written in the form "14.67×10").

Language is the supreme human "psychological tool," making higher forms of learning, problem-solving, and acquisition of many skills possible. And both Vygotsky and Dewey recognized that language is, primarily, a means of communication. The concepts and relationships captured in language are transmitted and acquired in a social medium.

In the child's early developmental experience, then, concepts (of "woman" or "man," for instance) come first, then the socially appropriate name or label for the concept is learned, with the help of more mature language users. In school, however, Vygotsky realized that children are taught some of the psychological tools of a society by being told their "names" (e.g., "exports," "energy," "social class," "capitalism," "Marxism") without the experience of the concepts. Unlike familiar and readily experienced objects (e.g., women and men), these concepts (e.g., exports or capitalism) are artifacts of a particular form of social life; they are not easy to learn about in direct ways. Nevertheless, it is these abstract and socially important psychological tools that we often try to teach in schools.

Vygotsky also recognized that a key factor in social learning was the young person's ability to learn by imitation. Interacting with adults and peers in cooperative social settings gave the young learner ample opportunity to observe, imitate, and subsequently develop higher mental functions.[11] This notion of imitation has been central in the work of researchers of our own day. In particular, Stanford psychologist Albert Bandura puts imitation at the center of his "social learning theory"—however, he gives it the somewhat more impressive label of "modeling":

Learning would be exceedingly laborious, not to mention hazardous, if people had to rely solely on the effects of their own actions to inform them of what to do. Fortunately, most human behavior is learned observationally through modeling: from observing others one forms an idea of how new behaviors are performed, and on later occasions this coded information serves as a guide for action. Because people can learn from example what to do, at least in approximate form, before performing any behavior, they are spared needless errors.[12]

According to Bandura, much learning of this type occurs when the child is engaged in everyday situations involving other people. Even when viewing TV and films, the young learner acquires much from the vicarious experience gained, and of course parents play a vital role as models in major areas such as language-learning.

Case Two

Consider this interaction between John and his father in the light of the points made by Dewey, Vygotsky, and Bandura about the social context of learning. What lessons are imparted during the social interaction? Evidently, John's father is modeling certain ways of "teaching" as a parent by giving John guidance about how he might make sense of an aspect of "government,"—that abstract name we give to the set of political arrangements we live under as defined in our Constitution. What is John learning and how is he learning it? Could this kind of learning happen in a classroom?

F: What are you watching on TV, John?

J: I was looking for basketball, Dad, but I got onto C-SPAN where they were broadcasting a debate from the Senate in Washington and I started watching it.

F: That's good. I hope this means you're going to become a lawyer and a politician instead of a basketball player.

J: Fat chance! —Well, maybe I'd settle for President! The debate has been interesting though. Come watch it with me. I've been puzzled by something.

F: What's that? The quality of our representation in Washington?

J: Stop kidding. I'm puzzled because it looks like the Vice President is there for the debate.

F: And?

J: Well, I thought the Vice President and the President only went to the Senate on very special occasions—like the, um, State of the Union Address, I think it's called.

F: You're right about the President, but not about the VP. Each have different constitutional duties, and one of the VP's duties is to preside over Senate debates.

J: Oh, that explains it then! I guess I was confused about what the Vice President is supposed to do. But, wait a minute, wasn't the VP away overseas last week? I remember seeing him on the news, visiting Australia.

F: Yes, that's right. What's the problem with that?

J: Well, how can he preside over the Senate if he is away a lot of the time?

F: The next in the line of authority takes over. I'm ashamed to say I'm not exactly sure who that is—I don't remember my civics lessons too well. Maybe it's the Senate Majority Leader. We should look it up somewhere.

J: Yeah, I think I brought home my American government textbook from school; I'll run up to my room and get it—it should tell us who's next in line.

F: OK, but hurry back. This debate looks interesting. It's about censorship and freedom of speech. Do you ever talk about those ideas in school?

Case Three

Strictly speaking, this is a case of discovery or inquiry rather than a case of learning, although of course the individuals involved ended by learning a great deal. Discuss the role played here by intellectual and even physical tools—would the investigators have learned what they did without these, or were these things ancillary to their problem-solving? What other resources available in our society or culture did these men draw upon? Would a lone individual have been able to make this breakthrough? Finally, does science education in our schools ever approximate what happened here?

The case involves two young scientists at the beginning of their careers, Francis Crick and James Watson, who shared an office in the Cavendish Laboratory at Cambridge University in the early 1950s. They got caught up in the worldwide "race" to decipher the structure of the molecule that is fundamental to life: DNA. This is an extract from the book by Watson describing the final stages in the breakthrough that won them the Nobel Prize. The two young men had been waiting for metal models of chemical compounds they believed to be ingredients of DNA to be prepared in the lab's workshop; but in the meantime they had been using rough cardboard cutouts to test their ideas about how to account for various kinds of data they had either collected or had been given, and the diverse calculations that they had made:

> Only a little encouragement [of the technicians in the workshop] was needed to get the final soldering accomplished in the next couple of hours. The brightly shining metal plates were then immediately used to make a model in which for the first time all the DNA components were present. In about an hour I had arranged the atoms in positions which satisfied both the x-ray data and the laws of stereochemistry. The resulting helix was right-handed with the two chains running in opposite directions. Only one person can easily play with a model, and so Francis did not try to check my work until I backed away and said that I thought everything fitted. . . . Another fifteen minutes of fiddling by Francis failed to find anything wrong, though for brief intervals my stomach felt uneasy when I saw him frowning. In each case he became satisfied and moved on to verify that another interatomic contact was reasonable. . . . The next several days were to be spent using a plumb line and a measuring stick to obtain all the relative positions of all atoms in a single nucleotide.[13]

Before discussing this case, you might want to reflect on the case "Learning to Balance Chemical Equations" in chapter 9. Both depend on social interactions for learning to take place.

Situated Cognition and Legitimate Peripheral Participation in Communities of Practice

The work of Vygotsky in the early decades of the twentieth century, and of Dewey and his friend George Herbert Mead, has inspired a number of contemporary scholars to develop further the idea that human thinking, learning, and problem-solving cannot usefully be regarded as processes that only involve the inside of the human cranium! We saw in Case Three above that the actual thinking processes of Crick and Watson involved the metal model of the large and complex DNA molecule—they were not only thinking *about* their model (and what it represented), but they were thinking *with* their model. Their thinking also involved talking (to each other, and to expert colleagues), moving about, manipulating rulers, frowning and muttering, looking up some laws of chemistry in advanced reference books, and so forth. Dewey captured this idea in a wonderful passage written in 1916, a passage that should be compulsory for teachers to know by heart:

> Upon this view, thinking, or knowledge-getting, is far from being the armchair thing it is often supposed to be. The reason it is not an armchair thing is that it

is not an event going on exclusively within the cortex or cortex and vocal organs. . . . Hands and feet, apparatus and appliances of all kinds are as much a part of it as changes within the brain.[14]

Over the past several decades, Michael Cole and his colleagues have carried out many studies of the ways in which young learners, in both school and other settings, actively draw upon the resources of their environments (including the expertise of their peers) when successfully solving meaningful problems or carrying out assignments. This work has led to the development of the notion of *situated cognition* or *situated learning*. What such students come to learn, and how they learn it, cannot be understood solely in terms of what cognitive processes are occurring inside their individual heads—learning occurs effectively, and naturally, in "situations" (a Deweyan notion) in which the student is located and actively engaged.

Jean Lave and Etiene Wenger have developed this notion even further. They studied examples—drawn from around the world, and involving different walks of life—where unskilled or unknowledgeable people learn quite complex bodies of knowledge and skills through their involvement in apprenticeships. Each of these apprentices learned by gradually becoming more and more steeped in a community of practice (becoming a tailor in Africa, becoming a quartermaster in the U.S. Navy, becoming a midwife in the Yucatan, among other examples). Starting as legitimate but peripheral members of a community of practice (the community of quartermasters on board a warship who do the navigating, for example), the apprentices—as they become more proficient—became full participants in the specialized life of their chosen field. Lave and Wenger strongly criticized the view that depicts learning as "internalization," as primarily a "cerebral process," and they stated:

> In contrast with learning as internalization, learning as increasing participation in communities of practice concerns the whole person acting in the world. Conceiving of learning in terms of participation focuses attention on ways in which it is an evolving, continuously renewed set of relations.[15]

We met some examples of this earlier: Young Oliver Twist was a peripheral participant in the community of practice constituted by Fagin and his band of pickpockets. Fortunately for Oliver, he was caught by the law before he became proficient and thus a full member of this community! Or, to move to a more uplifting example, Watson's book not only tells the story of the discovery of DNA, but also paints us a fascinating picture of how he moved from being a comparatively ignorant and awkward (and not to mention brash) legitimate but peripheral member of the community of scientists, to a fully participating and stellar member of this international community of practice. The example of Oliver Twist also illustrates another recent development in the idea of a community of learners. Fagin, the Dodger and others, and Oliver, formed a community engaged in learning things of importance to them. Brown and Campione[16] have developed this notion in the context of the schoolroom.

Culture and Learning

Thus far we have made frequent use of the terms "social" and "community," but we have avoided the related (but conceptually murky) notion of "culture." The noted anthropologist Clifford Geertz has suggested that there is no such thing as a common human nature shared by all individuals; humans are almost infinitely variable by nature, capable of developing in many different ways, and each of us is made what we are (our beliefs, our values, our tastes, our practices, our intellectual predispositions, and so forth) to a large degree by the culture into which we are born.[17] Clearly something as important as this must have major educational ramifications.

These days most teachers are forced to adjust to cultural differences in their classrooms; for one thing, students who have migrated as refugees across international borders often are culturally different. (Although one needs to be careful, for having been born and raised in a foreign country does not always indicate the presence of cultural differences—a student who has moved to the USA from Australia might be more at home in the culture of a middle-class predominately white school than a student who has moved to the same school from a Spanish-speaking area of Los Angeles, although many of the inhabitants of this latter region might be second or even third-generation Americans.) This example also illustrates the fact that there are major cultural differences within a large country like the USA; a typical urban school district might contain Samoan-Americans, Black and Hispanic Americans, Native Americans, Russian-Jewish Americans, third or fourth generation students of Anglo-American descent, and many others. And not all members of any one of these groups will necessarily share the same culture!

The important point for our purposes is that culture interacts in very complex ways with learning and the processes of schooling more generally. Understanding something about the culturally-shaped assumptions, practices, and values of students will enable a teacher to be more effective in promoting learning, but will also make the teacher more sensitive to his or her *own* deep-seated cultural assumptions and how these might be shaping the attitude that is being adopted towards students who seem to be "different".

There was a time (thankfully past?) when the poor performance on some school learning tasks by some culturally-different students was explained in terms of a so-called "deficit" model. The cultures these students brought to school with them were thought of as being in some sense "lower" on an evolutionary scale, as not containing resources that allowed these students to work effectively on learning tasks important for achieving success in the modern world. More recent research has revealed the complex truth—culturally-different students (while of course having individual differences, as is the case with respect to the members of any group) *do* have adequate resources and intellectual capacities, but this fact has been "masked" for many educators who are working from within a different cultural framework. Two examples might make this abstract point more concrete.

Shirley Brice Heath became interested in why minority children in a poor rural school district seemed unwilling—or maybe unable—to answer the routine kinds of questions asked by their teachers during typical school lessons.[18] She conducted interviews and observations, but also visited the teachers at home to document the kinds of questions that they asked their own children, and she compared these to the types of questions met with by the students in their homes. She discovered that teachers typically asked questions (both at school and in their own homes) *for which they knew the answers* (like "what is seven take away three?"), whereas this type of questioning was quite foreign to the students who—in their own culture—were asked about matters that the adult concerned did not usually know the answer to (like "why was Billy acting strange today?"). These students did not see the point of teacher-type questions, and had little practice at dealing with them, whereas the teachers' own children were well-socialized into this type of activity. There was no difference in intelligence here, no inability to answer questions, but rather there was a difference in cultural norms about the *point* of question-asking and question-answering behavior.

The second example is not unrelated; it is drawn from a rapidly expanding body of research by anthropologists, psychologists, and educators that focuses upon the fact that schooling embodies many practices and activities that reflect social or cultural values and proclivities and background knowledge that might not be shared by all students. Thus, some students might perform very well at tasks outside school, in culturally-familiar settings, while they fail miserably at school-based tasks that require (what appear to the teacher to be) the very same intellectual skills. In one study it was found that a student who was skilled at keeping scores for six players at once in ten-pin bowling matches (a complex activity that involves tracking "strikes" where the score on the next two bowls is added to the ten earned for the strike, and "spares" where the score on the next bowl is added to the ten for the spare) was quite unable to solve bowling score problems presented in the school setting.[19] (This phenomenon arises not only when there are cultural differences; it also can arise when adults who are competent problem-solvers in work settings are given similar problems to solve in school-settings!)

This discussion has obviously only scratched the surface of an important and complex topic. With respect to our major concern in the present book, however, Barbara Rogoff has summarized matters well:

> The structure of problems that humans attempt to solve, the knowledge base that provides resources, and the strategies for solution that are considered more or less effective or sophisticated are situated in a social matrix of purposes and values. The problems that are posed, the tools that are available to solve them, and the tactics that are favored build on the sociocultural definitions and technologies with which an individual functions.[20]

Before going on, you may find the case "Learning to Read" in chapter 9 interesting not only in the context of social learning but also as a way to think about many of the other theories already presented. The dialogue "Culture and Learning" in chapter 9 also raises issues worth thinking about.

Chapter 7

Cognitive Structures and Disciplinary Structures

One way to summarize the moral of the last couple of chapters is that there are two aspects of learning that have to be taken into account by a teacher: There are events happening in the individual "cognitive apparatus" of the learner as he or she struggles to understand, and remember, the subject matter that is being learned; but it is also the case that much, if not most, effective learning occurs in social settings, as learners communicate—or engage in collaborative activity—with other individuals. Furthermore, when a person learns, or develops or changes cognitively, these individual and social domains are intimately interrelated. As Newman, Griffin, and Cole put it when describing the content of their important book *The Construction Zone*,

> We take up the thesis that cognitive change [of the individual] is as much a social as an individual process. We examine the social interactions in which cognitive change is constructed so as to begin putting together a theory that shows how the individual and social worlds are entirely intertwined. We argue that to avoid dead ends in cognitive theory and educational practice, we have to go beyond citing individual factors and social factors as separable influences on cognitive change.[1]

While we are in sympathy with the general position of Newman, Griffin, and Cole, we believe there is still much to learn by considering what mechanisms are at work in the individual learner as he or she struggles to learn some new material—for we are confident that some understanding of these will be helpful to the teacher who is working with the learner or with groups of learners. Thus, in these next two chapters we are returning to the issues of how the subject-matter being learned is stored and structured in the memory of individual learners, and what a teacher can do to foster this learning process. And despite our critique of Piaget's relative lack of attention to the social context of learning, for our purposes here the analogy between the Piagetian child and mobile robot still seems quite fruitful.

Our fantasy robot would build up internal programs that govern its movements, and it would construct a "representation" of its surroundings in its internal data banks. Piaget seems to have had much the same picture of what happens as the exploring child develops its internal "structures," "schemata," and so on. But it is not clear how this account could apply to at least one form of learning that is of concern to teachers, namely, the gradual mastering by a young learner of disciplines like science, mathematics, and history. For in these cases the learner is only metaphorically "wandering around"—in learning a discipline, the student is not physically moving around in it, bumping into objects, and so forth.

The previous analogy still holds to a certain degree. The student *can* be regarded as constructing a kind of mental map of the subject (albeit with the help of teachers and others), a cognitive structure or internal representation that allows him or her to efficiently retrieve relevant information about the subject, to solve problems, and to learn new material and tie it in with what was previously known about the subject. If the wrong mental connections are made, we speak about the student being "lost" in the subject, just as when you are in a new town and incorrectly link the streets in your mind and literally get lost. If your mental map of the town is deficient, when you are given some new information (such as the location of a park), you incorporate it in a way that makes it even more difficult for you to travel around, understand what people are talking about, and so on. If you incorrectly "place" the park, you may have trouble understanding your friends when they talk about meeting outside the park near the theater. Similarly, the science student who has not properly linked matter and energy may have trouble in incorporating new material, such as material about the pressure exerted by light rays.

Maps and Organizers

In one of his early essays, John Dewey compared the studying of a discipline with the studying of a map. After wandering through some new terrain, an explorer produces a map; it is not intended to replace the thrill of the journey, the experience that other people will have if they explore the territory for themselves, but it does show the relationships among the main features they will encounter. The map gives future travelers a preliminary set of conceptions, and they can prepare for the dangers, but they can also integrate the various things that happen to them as they move about. And so it is with a discipline. The discipline has a "logic"; it has some key features that, if they are understood, will help the learner as he or she struggles to gain mastery. Again the map of a new town is a good analogy. If you have a general conception of the layout you can learn the details much more readily: "The streets are set in a rectangular grid, with the industrial part to the north and the sea to the south." One of the authors spent a considerable time lost in Canberra, the capital city of Australia, because he did not realize its "logic." A "model" city designed by American architect Burley Griffin, Canberra has its central streets laid out in large concentric circles. He kept wondering why he always ended up, after a long period of driving or walking, at the same place! How many students learning a subject like science or math have somewhat the same experience?

Psychologist David Ausubel has written a great deal about the point that is embodied in this map example: Learning is facilitated by presenting the student with "advanced organizers" or "anchoring ideas"—ideas that are fairly general and fairly basic to the topic about to be learned.

> These organizers are normally introduced in advance of the learning material itself and are used to facilitate establishing a meaningful learning set. Advanced organizers help the learner to recognize that elements of new learning materials can be meaningfully learned by relating them to specifically relevant aspects of existing cognitive structure.[2]

Whether or not, as a teacher, you always want to present advanced organizers to your students, you need to confront the moral in Ausubel's work: Students have to build up meaningful cognitive structures, and in one way or another you have to give them guidance as to the "mental connections" they should make both between the new ideas, and between the new ones and the old. (It is interesting to note that other cognitive psychologists call this creation of meaningful connections "webbing.")

Another analogy that we used earlier may be helpful here. Consider a research library that has just acquired several new volumes on the same topic. These would have to be shelved in appropriate places, perhaps crossreferenced with each other, and of course crossreferenced with the relevant volumes already in the library. Otherwise a user of the library might not be able to locate needed material without great inconvenience. Or consider the history teacher in the "periodization" case. If he wanted to change his strategy to an advanced organizer approach, he would have to present a meaningful scheme of periodization to his students first and then continue to connect facts and events to that scheme.

An Exercise

The fact that a learner is building an internal structure to represent the subject being studied, and the importance of this being done properly, can be demonstrated by trying the following exercise:

Interview a pupil who is trying to learn a new subject or topic and try to depict—preferably by constructing a diagram—the major features and interrelationships in the subject as he or she perceives them. While it is salutary to perform this exercise with a student who is having trouble with the subject, it is often even more salutary to do it with a student whom you regard as having mastered the material.

Now consider the following two examples that are along these same lines. They are taken from an actual experiment with fifth-grade children who had just been taught how light rays help us to see, and the pupils had also read the relevant chapter in a science textbook.[3] When asked to write a story to explain the phenomenon they had just learned about, one boy imagined himself as a light ray and wrote:

> One day the sun shoot me at a book which made some shadows. The book was removed and I went in a eye. The cornea was transparent when I went through the pupil then projected on to the retina and through the nerve in the brain.

It is apparent that this young scientist has not understood that light reflects from the object being seen and then into the eye; he has started to construct a faulty map of the relationships in the subject being studied—relationships between light, reflection, objects, and the pupil of the eye. Somewhat different misconceptions are apparent in the story written by a girl in the same class:

> When you read a book in good light such as a lamp, you see the words on the page. The words go in with the light through the cornea and through the pupil into the eye. The words are focused by the lens and then they form on the retina. Next the words are sent along the optic nerve to the brain. The brain then sends a message back to the eye telling you what you have just read.

In these examples, the faulty structures being built by the students have become obvious to the experimenters—and hopefully to the teacher—so that remedial action is possible. It is worth noting, however, that the errors the students are making are ones that the teacher might not have predicted. The ideas being taught are so familiar that a teacher might not realize how much difficulty the novice might have with them. In such cases the teacher might not detect the fact that a student is building a faulty structure, for unfortunately such structures are not like physical structures, open to public inspection. It might even happen that the student can get by and answer the teacher's questions in a vague way so that no one—not even the student—realizes that his or her cognitive structure embodies defects. (Ask students, individually, to diagram the cause of phases of the moon and wait for faulty but normally hidden assumptions to become apparent!) The cognitive scientist Donald Norman has written this (broadly constructivist) account of what often happens as a student in a class is confronted with new material:

> It is the student who decides what aspects of the material are important, what aspects are not. The student is essentially making up a story, and if the course material is not explicit enough, the student's story is apt to deviate considerably from what the instructor intended. But, because the student's story must be consistent with the course material, it is often an accurate characterization of what has been seen so far, and often it allows for consistent continued performance with new material. All this despite the fact that the structure is erroneous. This can lead to disaster, for when the student eventually has difficulties with the material, it may be at a spot far removed from the cause.[4]

Norman calls this the "Iceberg Model," for the danger lurks hidden well below the surface.

The Structure of Disciplines

Putting aside for the moment the issue of what is happening in the mind of the learner as a cognitive map or structure is being developed or constructed, what more can be said about the relationships within the subject or discipline that is being studied? Do disciplines like physics, chemistry, mathematics, geography, and literature have a structure? Are they like the planned city of Canberra, with a basic logic that, once it is comprehended, makes learning the details relatively easy? They certainly are *organized*. Their concepts, theories, techniques, and so on are certainly not a disorderly array. What bearing, if any, does this have upon the way a teacher should go about presenting them to students? (By phrasing the question this way we do not want to suggest that teachers always have to present material in a lecture format. All we wish to suggest is that the teacher has to make judgments about the way students might interact most effectively with the material.)

At various places in our earlier discussion we used the example of a student learning Einstein's theory, so let us look at this in a little more depth. How would you judge that one of your friends had learned—had really understood—this complex piece of science? Hopefully you would not be satisfied if he or she could only *recite* Einstein's famous equation $E = mc^2$. It is obvious that *reciting* the equation only shows that it has been remembered, it does not show that it has been understood. Most of us can remember an expression or phrase that we do not understand. This is a type of learning (rote memorization), but it is not the type we are considering here. It is possible that a parrot could be taught to say "$E = mc^2$," but this would not be an indication that avian physics is practicable, or that the Nobel Prize was likely to be awarded to a toucan!

To convince you that Einstein's theory had been learned, in the sense that we (and most school teachers) are interested in, your friend would most likely have to convince you about a number of things. First, he or she would have to show an understanding of Einstein's concepts—energy, mass, velocity of light, and mathematical notions like "square." To do this, your friend would have to show that he or she could *use* the concepts according to the rules of physics, for after all they *are* concepts of physics. Second, your friend would have to demonstrate an understanding of the evidence that supports the theory, the problems the theory solves, the theories it replaces, and so forth. In other words, your friend would have to demonstrate an understanding of many of the interrelationships in a large portion of the discipline of physics. These considerations suggest a similarity between the idea of structure being discussed here and the idea of conceptual structure that was discussed in chapter 5. Except there we were discussing the structure that was built up *inside the learner*, whereas here we are discussing the relation*ships inside the discipline or school subject*.

In short, then, learning a discipline seems to be learning about its "structure." Can this notion be made more precise?

Bruner, Schwab, and Hirst

The launching in 1957 of the first man-made satellite, the Russian Sputnik, had enormous impact on many aspects of life in the Western world. Education especially felt the impact. The methods of teaching in American schools came under increased critical scrutiny, and the curriculum became the focus for heated debate. Science educators, in particular, were faced with the issue of why the U.S.S.R. had been able to win the "space race," and in 1959 the National Academy of Science sponsored a conference that was held at Woods Hole, Massachusetts. Jerome Bruner, then a psychologist at Harvard, acted as conference chairperson, and he issued a report on the proceedings entitled *The Process of Education*.

One of the main problems Bruner addressed in his report was how the learning of science could be made more meaningful, in the sense that the student could be prepared by his or her training *now* to tackle problems in the *future*. The key to this type of learning lies, Bruner argued, in the student having grasped the *structure* of the discipline:

Grasping the structure of a subject is understanding it in a way that permits many other things to be related to it meaningfully. To learn structure, in short, is to learn how things are related. . . . In order for a person to be able to recognize the applicability or inapplicability of an idea to a new situation and to broaden learning thereby, he must have clearly in mind the general nature of the phenomenon with which he is dealing.[5]

The Woods Hole conference brought together leading scientists, educators, curriculum experts, and even some who were interested in the philosophy of science. While the notion of structure seemed to have played a prominent part in their discussions, it must be admitted that, at this stage, the notion was still rather murky.

By the early 1960s the notion had become more refined. In the United States Joseph Schwab wrote that the structure of a discipline could be analyzed into two parts: the substantive structure and the syntactical structure. The substantive structure, which Schwab also called the conceptual structure, is the structure

through which we are able to formulate a telling question. It is through the telling question that we know what data to seek and what experiments to perform to get those data. Once the data are in hand, the same conceptual structure tells us how to interpret them, what to make of them by way of knowledge. Finally, the knowledge itself is formulated in the terms provided by the same conception.[6]

On the other hand, the syntax of the discipline—its syntactical structure—concerns "what its canons of evidence and proof are and how well they can be applied."[7] Schwab was one of the driving forces behind the Biological Sciences Curriculum Study (BSCS) in the 1960s, where his ideas were very fruitfully put into practice. The BSCS curriculum stressed the syntax as well as the substance of biology.

At about the same time, Paul Hirst, a British philosopher of education, was thinking along similar lines. In effect he subdivided each of Schwab's two types of structure to produce a fourfold classification. According to Hirst:

(1)   [Each form of knowledge has] certain central concepts that are peculiar in character to the form. . . .

(2)   In a given form of knowledge these and other concepts . . . form a network of possible relationships in which experience can be understood. As a result a form has a distinctive logical structure. . . .

(3)   [A form of knowledge,] by virtue of its particular terms and logic, has expressions or statements . . . that in some way or other . . . are testable against experience. . . .

(4)   The forms have developed particular techniques and skills for exploring experience and testing their distinctive expressions. . . .[8]

Several examples might make these ideas clearer. There is an exercise in the biology curriculum where groups of students are each given a tray with a number of everyday objects—buttons, matches, coins, and so on—and they have to devise a classification scheme. Different groups of students, each with the same materials, produce different schema, and the subsequent discussion makes them realize that a classification is a man-made tool. Some classifications are more useful and more flexible than others, but all schemes are based on some underlying general idea or "logic." Armed with these insights the students are able to appreciate the modern biological classification of species—it is no longer a mysterious table handed down without rhyme or reason by the teacher and textbook.

Another example would be to take an exercise from physics that is designed for investigating the size of a molecule. Students count the number of drops of oil falling from a graduated dropper and find how many drops make up, say, a cubic centimeter. This gives them a rough figure for the volume of a drop. (If there are twenty drops in 1 cc, for example, then each drop is about one-twentieth, or about .05, of a cc.) One drop is then allowed to fall into a large dish of calm water, and time is given for it to spread out into a large circular patch. The dimensions are measured, and the surface area is easily calculated using the formula $A = \pi r^2$. (Suppose the circular patch is about twenty centimeters in diameter, in which case its area is about 320 square centimeters.) Then, on the assumption that the patch is a very thin cylinder (of unknown but small thickness), the thickness can be calculated using the simple formula:

volume of cylinder = area of the top × the height or thickness

The volume is known (in our example it was .05 cc, the volume of the drop that was allowed to spread out), and the area of the top of the oil patch was calculated from the measurements to be 320 square centimeters. The height or thickness is thus .05/320, or .00016 cm. On the assumption that the oil patch cannot be less than one oil molecule thick, although of course it might be several, this gives the student a figure for the maximum size of a molecule. In this way the concept of a molecule becomes more alive, and the student also gains some insight into the way measurement and calculation are wonderful tools for the scientist. Physics and mathematics are seen to be in fruitful relationship.

One final aspect of the work of Schwab and Hirst needs to be mentioned. Both raised the issue of how many disciplines actually exist, and Hirst was bold enough to give an answer. He claimed that there were only seven "forms of knowledge" that had the four types of structure he had described: mathematics, physical sciences, human sciences, history, religion, literature and the fine arts, and philosophy. (Later, reacting to criticism, he revised this list somewhat.) Hirst also recognized that there were some "domains" —subjects that had a combination of several forms of knowledge. Geography is a good example of this, for it is a mixture of human sciences, physical sciences, and so on.

An Evaluation

What is to be made of the notion of the "structure of knowledge" or the "structure of a discipline"? There has been a great deal of negative discussion, especially among philosophers of education. It is not at all clear that a discipline like physics has *a* structure. To stick with Hirst's formulation, it is not clear that it has central concepts, for the discipline can be ordered in various ways, each way having its own central concepts. In other fields the problem is even more acute—think of psychology, where there are many rival theories like Freudianism, Skinnerianism, and so forth. It is far from clear that, whatever concepts and techniques and tests against experience Freudian psychoanalysis has, Skinnerian behaviorism has the same. And it is not at all apparent that a field like literature has a "structure" at all. Finally, both Hirst and Schwab seem to separate the concepts of a discipline from its methodology. This is the essence both of Schwab's two categories, and of the top and bottom halves of Hirst's fourfold table of criteria. But the validity of the separation can be questioned. The methodology of a discipline is so much affected by the concepts and theories that are current that the attempt to separate them is completely artificial.[9]

Even if Schwab and Hirst got the details wrong (and they are important details), the spirit of their work seems unassailable. Basically they treat disciplines as "living" entities, as bodies of knowledge that are in constant flux, growing and changing, and with which the student has to learn to work. And to work with a discipline one has to have a "feel" for its dynamics, and some "mental map" of it. One has to have a sense of where the knowledge claims of the discipline come from, and how they are evaluated. In sum, one has to abandon the "cold storage" view of knowledge that John Dewey made us sensitive to and view knowledge as a human construction designed to make sense of experience. So, then, as a *heuristic* idea—a notion that points us in an educationally fruitful direction—the notion of the structure of a discipline as developed by Bruner, Schwab, and Hirst seems well worth keeping.

To pursue further the idea of structure, you might want to consider "Learning Facts and Structures" in chapter 9. You might also try to apply the ideas of Schwab and Hirst to the case, "Justifying Lab Sessions."

Chapter 8

The Cognitive Science
Approach

By this stage you might have decided that we have overused the crude example of a mobile computerized robot. Our motives were pure—we wanted a dramatic way to illustrate the notions of cognitive structure with mental maps, prerequisites for learning, cognitive developmental stages, and so forth. However, for many contemporary educational and psychological researchers the computer is no mere analogy. It has become a scientific working hypothesis. There are strong and weak versions of this hypothesis, with corresponding research programs. The strong program is termed strong not because it is necessarily more valid but because its claims are more extreme. Unlike the proponents of the weak program, who assume that mind and brain are very much *like* a computer, adherents to the strong program believe that the brain *is* a computer—made up of protein molecules rather than silicon chips. This general orientation to psychology, encompassing both programs, goes under a variety of names, most commonly "the information processing approach" and "the cognitive science approach." Its essence is captured in the following extract from one of the early texts in the field:

> Computers take symbolic input, make decisions about the recoded input, make new impressions from it, store some or all of the input, and give back symbolic output. By analogy, that is most of what cognitive psychology is about. It is about how people take in information, how they recode and remember it, how they make decisions, how they transform their internal knowledge states, and how they translate these states into behavioral outputs. . . . As a consequence of coming to know computer science, cognitive psychologists now theorize about human capacities and behavior using concepts such as input, output, storage, buffer, executive processor, and system architecture.[1]

In a much more recent paper Richard Meyer pointed out that "although the model has been amended, modified, and effectively challenged, the description of the architecture of the mind remains as a central tenet of information-processing psychology."[2] There seems little doubt that the "architecture of the mind" largely depends upon (is "supervenient" upon, philosophers would say) brain architecture, just as the powers of a computer in part depend upon the architecture of its chips and wiring. Great headway is being made in deciphering the neural structure of the brain; for example, abnormalities in neural "wiring" that seem to be responsible for some forms of dyslexia (and the attendant learning problems) have been discovered, and the relevant nerve pathways have been remediated using computer-based exercises that in essence retrain the relevant portion of the brain. However, it seems extremely unlikely that most of the failures to learn met in typical classrooms can be attributed to faulty neural architecture. Our concern here is with the computer model of learning, not with the technicalities of wiring!

The Heuristic Value for Researchers

As hinted above, the information-processing or cognitive science model has great suggestive or heuristic power, and it has been able to focus the attention of researchers onto some very fruitful issues. In other words, whether or not the human brain *is* computer-like, this model gives us an interesting perspective to use when we look at human learning. Consider what happens when you start to use a personal computer. You type information into the machine via the keyboard, and as each key is struck the information is "encoded" or changed into the form of an electrical pulse. The computer is wired internally so that the corresponding information is recorded in its "working memory"; after you have edited or rearranged the message you have typed in, you may instruct the computer to permanently "remember" the message by storing it in a file on a disk. This model suggests that it might be interesting to determine if humans also have a "working" memory and a more permanent "long-term" memory. And—surprise!—it turns out that they do.

In comparison to a computer, human working or short-term memory is very limited, for the average person can remember only about seven unrelated items at one time (the "unrelated" is important, for if the information can be chunked together into meaningful groupings then more can be handled). It is a common experience to look up a phone number and to have forgotten it by the time one gets around to dialing. Where humans seem to do better than computers is with respect to permanent storage capacity. For example, one author's older laptop computer uses a 3½ inch "floppy disk" that is limited to storing 1.4 megabytes (MB), and possesses a "hard disk" that can handle only about 20 MB; new hard disks and CD-ROMs can store more data. However, it is believed that the human brain has a practically limitless storage capacity because information seems to be stored at the molecular level, and there are a great many molecules. The way in which information gets transferred from short-term into long-term memory is a related, interesting avenue of research, and so is the issue of how it is encoded into short-term memory in the first place.

Besides the structure of memory, many other leads have been opened up by this general approach. For one thing, a floppy disk can hold a limited number of files (although storing an encyclopedia on disk is an impressive accomplishment), and there is an index on each disk that automatically registers the name of each new file as it is set up, and its location on the disk. But how is new information stored in the cognitive apparatus of the learner? How is it indexed so that the learner can quickly retrieve it when needed? For instance, what is the storage for the information that a platypus is a strange mammal found in Australia? Is it "filed" under "animals" or under "mammals," so that the individual who needs to retrieve the information has to mentally (and perhaps not consciously) search through a long "list" of data? Is it somehow "cross listed" with "aquatic animals" and "fur-bearing animals"? Or is it in its own individual file: "amphibious egg-laying mammal with a duckbill"? Is any light shed on the nature of your own "filing system" by your answer to the following question: How do you go about trying to remember something you have forgotten, such as the name of an old acquaintance? What is the significance of the feeling that "it's just on the tip of my tongue"? Does this mean you have just about located the proper mental file?

Cognitive scientists generally model the human memory as a complex network in which each piece of data is cross-linked (or cross-indexed) to many others—a model that squares with what we know about how neurons in the brain are cross-connected in incredibly complex ways. So-called "neural network" devices now are being built to mimic this arrangement.

Another issue is that most computers available commercially process material serially, that is, in one linear sequence. It is not clear that humans suffer from this serious limitation. There is some evidence that we are able to engage in parallel processing. It is very useful to be able to put a problem "at the back of your mind" while you go about solving something else, only to find later on that in the meantime the original problem also has been solved. The present authors are sad to report that their capacities to do this seem to be diminishing over the years!

As the final example of the suggestive power of the information-processing model (at least of the weak program), it is clear that the personal laptop computer being used to produce the draft of the present chapter is not as powerful as the large computers at Stanford and Columbia universities. On the other hand, this PC cannot do the graphics and sound recording that can be handled by the machines belonging to some of our children (for the relevant chips have never been installed). Can the differences between these computers throw light on the differences between individual humans? Some people are gifted at art or music or math, but are less able in other subjects; some students get the drift of new school work very quickly, while others have to struggle with it. Headway is being made with such issues, but there are still many uncertainties. There is, however, some evidence that differences in ability are not so much associated with differences in brute "computing power" as they are with the amount of experience and acquaintance the individuals have had with the areas in which they are solving problems, and with their mental "flexibility"—their ability to switch from one methodology to another until they arrive at one that is suitable for handling the problem. In other words, less successful problem solvers seem to stick with a fruitless approach or "program" much longer than is optimal, while successful solvers quickly detect whether or not the method they first adopted is working and, if it is not, they change to some other strategy. This is a finding that, if it is borne out, has obvious importance for teachers. It suggests that they might be doing their students a great service by giving encouragement to try a diversity of methods when tackling problems. As McKeachie puts it:

> The effectiveness of student learning depends to some extent upon the strategy used by the student. Students often fail to choose the strategy that they can use most effectively and also fail to match their strategy to the learning task. This suggests two tasks for teachers: (1) teaching students to identify their own most effective learning strategies; and (2) teaching students how to use a larger repertoire of methods of learning.[3]

The Heuristic Value for Teachers

Our last example is merely one of many that could be presented to show that the weak program within the cognitive science or information-processing model has many insights to offer teachers as well as researchers. A number of these were also touched upon in earlier chapters. Draw your own lessons about teaching and learning from the following:

- A person working with a small computer (and especially an older model) soon realizes that there is a limit to how quickly information can be fed into the machine—its coding capacity can become overloaded.
- One cannot get a computer to do something it has not been programmed to do.

- The computer has to be instructed how to file the new material. (Most personal computers are programmed so that if the user forgets to give a precise file name, the machine will use some "default" name of its own.)
- To retrieve information that the computer has stored, the precise wording has to be used. If the user gives an incorrect file name, then the "wrong" file (from the user's point of view) will be produced.
- To get a computer to solve a problem or carry out a task, the work has to be properly sequenced, and the rules necessary to solve the problem must be precisely formulated. (This is the thrust of much technical work in the strong program, which to date has been fully successful only with relatively straightforward tasks.)
- If you give the computer the wrong instructions, or a muddled task, then there is usually a great deal of internal activity (as indicated by the spinning of disk drives and flashing of lights), culminating in the appearance on the monitor screen of an "error message."
- If the computer was not able to carry out a task you set it, the fault is more likely to have been *yours* rather than the machine's.
- Most computers are unable to automatically switch from one program to another that is more appropriate for the task at hand; the person using the computer has to take a guiding role.
- To program a computer, you have to use a language that it "understands." A computer that is not equipped (by engineering or by "training") to deal with a particular programming language will not respond to commands given in that language.
- A computer will not be able to carry out some complex operation you have set it, if you keep interfering with its operation (by interrupting its processing by typing in new instructions or data).

An important issue arises here. Your reaction to these items might be that, interpreted as pieces of advice, they are all sound but they are all matters of common sense. Is this all that is involved in teaching? Undoubtedly common sense—which often is a scarce ingredient—plays an important part. Some people have argued that humans have been teaching each other since the origin of our species, and if we were not naturally good at it we would have become extinct. It is instructive to reflect on the fact that dealing with a computer is partly a matter of common sense as well, but it is staggering how many people on first exposure become terrified or overwhelmed and throw good sense aside. Thirty children can be equally as terrifying to the new teacher as a computer is to a novice user, and the terror can last longer!

Furthermore, common sense is not the whole of the story. It certainly helps, in using a computer, to know even a little about how it operates, about the internal "architecture," and so on. And it is also necessary to know quite a bit about the tasks you want the machine to perform. Similarly, in teaching children you undoubtedly are assisted by knowing something about the psychology of learning, and by having a deep understanding of the subjects you want the students to learn. John Dewey again put it well; he said that the task of the teacher was to "psychologize" the material the student was to learn. And educational psychologist Lee Shulman talks of the "subject matter knowledge for teaching" that expert teachers possess—they know the difficulties that learners can have with specific portions of the subject matter, and they have a stock of ideas about how to help students overcome these difficulties. This means, for example, that the math teacher has to know enough about the subject to see where the student is heading, and enough about the principles of human learning to be able to lay out or structure the material in such a way that the student will be able to fruitfully interact with it. It is a noble image, made no less noble by the fact that common sense plays an important part.

Some Deficiencies of the Computer Model

It is unwise in science and technology to say "never" or "not possible." Many things that seemed impossible to the people of one age later became commonplace. It is possible for heavier-than-air machines to fly, it is possible for humans to reach the moon, and it is possible to transplant organs. Maybe, then, computers will eventually be able to do things that currently seem to be in the realm of fantasy. Nevertheless, as it stands at the present moment, the computer or information-processing model has clear limitations—there are aspects of human learning that it does not adequately capture, especially the strong program. (Which is why, in our discussions in this book, we have almost always drawn only on the work within the weak program.)

One important deficiency is that the model leaves out the tremendous influence of "affective factors," such things as interest, motivation, and emotion. We all know how hard it is to concentrate on anything but the simplest tasks when we are emotionally distraught, and we all have experienced the way our good judgment suffers when we are angry. It is very difficult to get a miserable or angry student to learn very much.

On the other hand, many of us have had the exciting experience of working at a deeply interesting task (if not our studies, perhaps one of our hobbies) for a time that we thought was only a few minutes but turned out to be many hours—witness the old saying "time flies when you are having a good time." Learning seems to be no effort when interest is present, though John Dewey reminds us that the interest has to be *intrinsic* interest and not mere "sugar-coating" having nothing to do with the nature of the learning task. (This is not to deny, however, that reinforcement and reward can play an important activating role.)

Present-day computers do not display emotion, they do not seem to be able to get interested in the task at hand, they do not seem to be affected by positive reinforcement, and—very importantly, given the discussion in chapter 6—they cannot learn from their social environment. In these respects the computer model of learning is defective. Researchers in the information-processing tradition, however, are well aware of the issues here, and they are hard at work.

Another factor that clearly influences learning, but is not yet readily absorbable into the model, is "self-concept." To use a common example, some students perceive themselves as being very poor at mathematics. This self-judgment, whether an accurate assessment or not, certainly influences their performance. On the other hand, a computer does not have a view of its own prowess, or if it does it keeps it to itself and its opinion does not affect the way it works! The alert teacher can take steps to remedy this situation with respect to a student, and here the computer analogy does shed some light. A particular type of PC might not, according to a user, be much good for a certain task. And, of course, it might not be. But perhaps the problem is in how the PC is being used—perhaps the correct program has not been inserted, or perhaps not enough effort has been expended in trying to solve the task using a variety of alternative methods ("there is more than one way to skin a cat"). Similarly, a teacher might help a student to overcome a low self-evaluation by showing that there are reasonable alternative hypotheses as to why he or she is struggling with math—perhaps some fundamental knowledge has been missed, or perhaps the student has not tried hard enough, or perhaps the student has let emotion cloud his or her judgment. (The problem, of course, is that once a learner blames lack of success on low ability, it undercuts further efforts to master the subject—it is usually thought that trying harder will not help if one simply is out of one's intellectual depth.)

It is also clear, as we mentioned above, that computers are far from being "social" entities. As we discussed in chapter 6, humans are born into a society where they learn an enormous amount from others, chiefly through the medium of language that allows intellectual interaction and engagement to occur, but also through working collaboratively in a "community of learners." We tend to think of computers as "stand alone," asocial machines; even if they are networked, as in a large office and in some schools, they are still more like individuals who happen to have a common link rather than being like the inherently social members of a human culture. However, we should remember that even those computers that can perform complex tasks, do so because they are following an ingenious *program*; and such programs *are* produced by humans who are members of a society—there is a social aspect to computers (and programs) that is often overlooked because it is beneath the surface. (There is an analogy that might be helpful here: Robinson Crusoe is sometimes thought of as being a man who was living in complete isolation from society, cast away on his desert island. But it is impressive how many of the trappings of civilization he actually had with him or that he strived to reproduce; he was a man who was shaped to his core by social factors!)

Finally, we must emphasize that most present-day computers are immobile (although many are portable). Although they may undergo a great deal of internal activity, they are physically stationary and inert. In our earlier discussions we used the analogy of a *mobile* computer or robot, and we tried to make clear that this was not merely for dramatic effect. The human learner is active, both physically and mentally, and this activity seems to be a vital ingredient in the learning process. John Dewey stressed that it is wrong to think of physical and mental activity as two unrelated things; the words "physical" and "mental" are distortions—the learner's physical activity is suffused with the mental, and vice versa. Our discussions of the work of Dewey, Piaget, Köhler, Lave and Wenger, and Newman, Griffin, and Cole, should have underscored this general point.

But while the information-processing model unfortunately draws our attention away from the importance of physical activity and social engagement, it has the positive virtue of reminding us in a very vivid way of the mental activity that takes place in the learner. Donald Norman writes:

> What goes on in the mind of the learner? A lot: People who are learning are active, probing, constructing. People appear to have a strong desire to understand. The problem is that people will go to great lengths to understand, constructing frameworks, constructing explanations, constructing huge edifices to account for what they have experienced. . . . But . . . a learner builds on incomplete evidence.[4]

Understanding, Meaning, and the "Chinese Room"

There is one remaining issue that is brought to the forefront by the information-processing model—a matter so crucial it deserves discussion in a separate section. A major difference between humans and computers (or at least, computers as they are at present) lies in the fact that computers can store and later retrieve any information that can be fed in, whether this information is simple or complex, meaningful or nonsensical. Humans, on the other hand, are far-and-away at their best with material that is *meaningful* to them. (The exception to this is the category of savants, as depicted in the well-known film *Rainman*: Some savants can perform prodigious feats of memory with material that they do not comprehend.)

It seems not to matter to a computer what is being transferred to its hard disk; the information will be filed and stored for easy retrieval. With humans, *understanding* something like Einstein's theory makes a great difference to its learnability and rememberability—meaningless or poorly understood items are difficult to remember, and seem to be poorly networked or connected to other items.

It is far from clear what is involved in understanding, or in making information meaningful; those investigators who follow the strong program often try to downplay this issue, and even claim that it is a metaphysical matter with which genuine cognitive science does not have to grapple.[5] This reaction seems largely due to the fact that, while it is possible to program a computer to *follow* (i.e., run according to) rules, we don't know where to start in order to program the computer so that it will *understand* the rules it is following. So it is tempting for followers of the strong program to claim that there is *nothing* more than following rules—that the ability to follow rules is all we mean by "understanding the rules," and that a separate state of understanding is a mere "will-o'-the-wisp."

The philosopher John Searle has devised a famous (and still controversial and widely discussed) example to illustrate his argument that because a computer can follow rules (a program) it does *not* imply that it understands the *meaning* of what it is doing. Searle imagined that a man, who does not understand Chinese, was inside a room where a question written in Chinese was passed in through a slot; the man had to look up each Chinese character (meaningless to him) in a rule book written in English, and then take other Chinese characters meaningless to him out of marked boxes and pass these back through the slot in the order specified by the rule book. The room with the man in it (the "Chinese Room") is, essentially, analogous to a large computer—the input is a question, the output is an answer generated by the operation of the rule book or program. But, as Searle insists, "neither the person inside nor any other part of the system literally understands Chinese," and because a "programmed computer has nothing this system does not have, the programmed computer . . . does not understand Chinese either."[6] The point is that the man in the Chinese Room generates a product that makes it seem that he *can* understand

Chinese, but the understanding occurs in the mind of the programmer (presumably a bilingual person) who wrote the rulebook. (In this example, of course, the man in the room is able to follow the rulebook because he can speak English; a real computer does not even understand the program it is following, for in essence the program reduces to a lot of "open" or "shut," or "on" or "off" commands that, via wired-in circuits, control electronic "gates.")

To see the importance of understanding and meaning in human learning, carry out the following experiment on a friend who has not read this portion of the book.

1. Give your friend a sheet of paper and a pencil, and then read to him or her this passage, without saying it is a poem:

   > There was a young man from Australia
   > Who painted his face like a dahlia
   > A bee passing by
   > Pollinated his eye
   > So the experiment, you see, was no failure.

   Now get your friend to write down as much of this as he or she can remember.

2. Then repeat the procedure with the following, again making no comment about it:

   > Cloud sin a was packet marble and
   > Who mud the pan elephant card sky
   > On idea money tiger
   > Reinforcement gift film
   > Thus paper breakfast, my sorry, shawl on ideals.

3. Finally, after your friend has finished writing as much of the second "poem" as can be remembered, ask him or her to try to think of the last limerick that had been come across even if it was a long time ago.

One of the authors has tried this "experiment" a number of times, with large groups, and the results have always been the same. Almost all people in the group remember the first poem—not all of them get it perfectly correct, but all come close and the meaning of the poem is preserved. (Once or twice a person who did not know that a dahlia is a flower had difficulties.) Almost nobody gets more than a few odd words of the second nonsense "poem"—which is of the same length, and indeed most people give up trying by the end of the second line! Quite a number of people, but not all, quickly respond that the poem about the colorful Aussie was the most recent limerick they had heard—even though the first poem was never identified as a limerick by the experimenter, and was not even called a poem!

This odd exercise seems to illustrate that people can fairly easily remember something with meaning, as opposed to something without meaning; and that they immediately start making mental connections and categorizations of the meaningful material. (Evidently some people's memories connect the first poem mentally with the category of limericks, and no doubt they file it away under the category of "Australia" as well.) Recall Donald Norman's words quoted at the end of the previous section—people have a strong drive to understand, and mentally they are very active when learning.

Another example of the drive to understand, displayed by people but not by computers, comes from the work of the mathematics educator S.H. Erlwanger.[7] He was studying a class of sixth-graders who were using Individually Prescribed Instruction (IPI) Mathematics, and he came across a student, Benny, whom the teacher regarded as being above average. Erlwanger struck up a conversation with Benny, and soon found that the young man had some serious misunderstandings of fractions and decimals (the topics currently being studied). In most exercises, Benny could add fractions and multiply decimals correctly, and yet he said that $2/1 + 1/2$ was equal to 1, and that $2/10$ expressed as a decimal was 1.2. Further investigation showed that Benny regarded $400/400$ as equal to 8.00, and that both $1/9$ and $4/6$ were equal to 1. (The fact that such different fractions yielded the same result was no puzzle to Benny, for he argued—correctly—that in math quite different forms exist for the same number, and he seemed to regard $1/9$ and $4/6$ as being a case in point!)

Benny, it turns out, had invented a set of rules for himself, that made sense of the problems he was working on. The problem was that these rules, which frequently led to the wrong answer, often also led to the correct one. The teacher (who, in IPI, was only looking at the answers and not at the student's reasoning) did not realize that anything was seriously wrong. So Benny was occasionally reinforced by the teacher, and he became convinced that his understanding was fine. Benny explained right away the occasions when he got an apparently incorrect answer by the argument outlined earlier—the teacher or the textbook had merely stated the correct answer in a different form than the one he had used.

The case of Benny is a fine example of what Donald Norman called the "Iceberg Model" of mind (see chapter 7). The tip of Benny's mental iceberg was correct often enough that the teacher did not detect any problems; but beneath the surface and hidden from view, Benny's understanding was seriously deficient, until Erlwanger took the time to get Benny to explain his ideas. Even so, Benny was not operating with meaningless material—he had invented his own set of rules and meanings, so that the material made sense to him! Erlwanger argues, with some justice, that this is a general problem with programs of individual instruction—a judgment that would be endorsed by Dewey and Vygotsky, who believed that working as part of a social group was an effective way to help learners make correct and fruitful mental connections and corrections. It seems reasonable to believe that Benny probably would never have gone off on the wrong track if he had to explain and defend his ideas to a group of other students (or to the teacher).

Plato and the Mind

There are several loose ends to be dealt with. In the first place, where do we stand with respect to Plato's problem? How does the cognitive science model resolve it?

To find the answer, let us go back to the personal computer with which the manuscript of this book was prepared. When first switched on, it "knows" almost nothing. This particular PC has a smidgen of inborn knowledge built-in at the factory. But the PC is so wired, so constructed, that it has great potential—it has built-in powers just awaiting some data to work on, and awaiting the right program or instructions to be fed in; when it was purchased, we had to decide what word-processing program to install. In this respect the PC is a good model for the current view of a child. The child comes into the world prewired with the neurophysiological equipment and social propensities that will make learning possible. The child also has a little in the way of inborn programming—some reflexes that give it a primitive capacity to start interacting with the environment (sucking, crying, smiling, and so on). There is one further, very important parallel: The PC has a wired-in "computer language" or "machine language," without which it would not be able to "comprehend" the programs or data that are going to be fed into it. (Just think of what happens when a program is inserted into the PC—it would just be a jumble of electrical impulses unless the computer had the capacity to "know" what to do with them—you will note the figurative language here.) Similarly, psychological theorists like Jerry Fodor believe—controversially—that the child must be born with a prewired "language of thought," otherwise it would not be able to process the information that it receives. For instance, without this inborn primitive language, the child would not be able to record or think about or process the words it hears its mother speaking. Indeed, they would not be words at all to the baby. Thus, for Fodor, this "language of thought" is not English or any other national tongue. Fodor writes, in a passage that is sure to remind you of our earlier discussions of Plato:

> One cannot learn a first language unless one already has a system capable of representing the predicates in that language *and their extensions*. And, on pain of circularity, that system cannot be the language that is being learned. But first languages *are* learned. Hence, at least some cognitive operations are carried out in languages other than natural languages.[8]

To make a long and complex matter short, then, Plato presently stands as somewhat vindicated. Learning *is* only possible because some prior things are known. This is not quite the way Plato set up his original dilemma, of course, but he came close!

The second loose end can be handled quickly. It is simply necessary to issue a warning: The notion of structure, both when used to refer to the structure of knowledge or of a discipline and when used to refer to cognitive structures, is *metaphorical*. A structure is familiarly a solid entity, such as building or scaffold. But whatever they are, cognitive and knowledge structures are not solid or spatial. The parts of a scaffold are spatially related, whereas the parts of a cognitive or knowledge structure are logically or perhaps psychologically related (and to make this latter notion clearer would really involve opening the proverbial "can of worms"). You need to be extremely careful not to be misled, not to ask inappropriate questions— for instance, the sorts of questions that would be sensible only about something spatial.

Finally, our extended use of the computer analogy obliges us to address the issue of whether we are implying that humans are nothing more than machines—that they are "hardware" or bodies, and that they do not have a mind or soul. If one inclines to the latter view (that is, to the dualistic view that a person consists of a body and mind in interaction—a venerable view going back to antiquity), can one consistently use the parallel with a computer? The issues here are under lively contemporary debate—as illustrated by the work of John Searle on our mysterious ability to understand meanings—but it is clear that while *any* position you are likely to hold has difficulties, it is possible that the computer analogy is compatible with a range of views. Certainly it seems to be compatible both with the view that a person is only a machine (the "physicalist" position) and with the dualist position. Whether or not present day computers have an internal mental life and are able to achieve understanding, or whether in the future complex computers will be produced that do have such features, there is little doubt that our human capacity to think and to learn depends upon the neurological hardware that we possess, and the "programming" that our parents, teachers, and peers provide us. The parallel with a computer helps to throw light on these things, so it would be foolhardy to throw it out—the weak program is very useful heuristically, at least. We just need to be aware that, like any scientific model, the computer or information processing model might not throw light on *all* human phenomena.

In the next chapter, the cases "Learning Theory and Artificial Intelligence" and "Learning to Balance Chemical Equations" are relevant to the issues raised in this chapter.

This ends our discussion. We rest our case about learning theories, the three blind men and the elephant, and the need for teachers to be aware of different ways to think about learning. We invite you to try out what you have learned by engaging in the arguments and issues we have provided in the final chapter of this book.

Chapter 9

Arguments and Issues

Up to this point, we have described a number of theories of learning, and by the use of cases, examples, questions, and critiques we have tried to get you to think about each theory as you were learning about it. In this last chapter we will offer a series of vignettes and additional cases mostly in the form of imaginary dialogues, disputes, arguments, and debates that we hope will get you to think even more deeply and broadly about the nature of learning. They may be used selectively as the basis for class discussions or you just may want to browse through them on your own and wrestle with the puzzles they present. The first eleven vignettes are closely related to the earlier chapters and were recommended for consideration near the end of each chapter. The others treat more general issues about learning or focus attention on practical applications of learning theory. The last vignette, "A Problem with Multiple Theories of Learning," forces some important reflection about this book as a whole.

As you read these vignettes you will see that they are not just straightforward examples of the theories that have been treated. The real world is not as simple as all that. Of necessity, textbooks and courses artificially separate aspects of the business of educating to make studying them easier, as we have done in this book on learning theories. In the work of the professional educator, however, concerns about learning often have woven into them real life concerns about curriculum and aims, teaching strategies, professional ethics, personal beliefs and values, and even political considerations. The cases and dialogues that follow open the door to such considerations and a thorough discussion of them with others should bring to life the complexities of the real world of educating while stimulating your thinking about learning. To give you an overview of the topics that have been treated and the major points at issue, we have provided a summary in table 1.

TABLE 1. Summary of Arguments and Issues

Page	Title*	Issue
91	The Relation of Learning Theory to Teaching (1)	What innate knowledge or equipment is necessary for humans to be able to learn?
91	Different Kinds of Learning? (1)	Are there different kinds of learning?
92	A Starting Place for Learning (2)	What innate knowledge or equipment is necessary for humans to be able to learn?
93	Learning and Behavior Change (3)	Does learning always produce a change in behavior?
94	The Scientific Status of Gestalt and Behaviorist Theories (4)	What makes a theory scientific? Are only scientific theories useful?
96	Different Teaching-Learning Strategies (4)	How does what is learned become meaningful to the learner?
96	Teaching, Learning, and Stages of Development (5)	If minds develop naturally, can teaching accelerate the process?
97	Learning to Read (6)	How many learning theories can be applied to reading?
98	Learning Facts and Structures (7)	What is the structure of a subject?
99	Learning Theory and Artificial Intelligence (8)	Are computers models for minds or are minds models for computers?
99	Learning to Balance Chemical Equations (8)	How are complex computational processes learned?
101	The Evaluation of Verbal and Skill Learning	How do we judge if students have learned?
102	Learning the Meaning of Adding	Is being able to add the same as understanding what addition is?
103	Learning Shakespeare	Can appreciation be taught and learned?
104	Learning Responsibility	Can responsibility be learned and measured?
105	Culture and Learning (6)	How does culture affect teaching and learning?
106	Individualized Learning	Does getting a worksheet right mean that learning has taken place?
107	A Problem with Multiple Theories of Learning	Aren't different theories about the same thing either right or wrong?

*A number in parentheses after a title indicates that that case has been recommended to be used in conjunction with a specific chapter.

The Relation of Learning Theory to Teaching

A: I think that as long as you know something about learning theory, then you ought to be able to teach.

B: You also have to know the subject matter you're going to teach, don't you?

A: Yes, of course, but that isn't enough. I've had teachers who really knew their math or history who really weren't very good at teaching me math or history.

B: OK, then we agree; you need to have both a knowledge of the subject matter and a knowledge of learning theory.

C: No you don't. Think about it. You do have to know your subject matter because you can't teach what you don't know. But you don't need to know learning theory to be able to teach. Think of all the mothers and fathers in the world who teach children things without knowing any learning theory at all.

A: But they use implicit learning theories, don't they? I mean some parents think they get you to learn things by reward and punishment, by a kind of operant conditioning, and some just naturally act as if children learn best through their own experience, like Dewey's problem solving. Some are really Lockean, keeping it real simple and repetitive until the complex associations are made.

C: But having an implicit learning theory is different than having explicit theories at hand. Having an implicit theory is limiting; it's nonreflective. You don't know why you're doing what you're doing when you teach, you just do it and it learning doesn't result, you just keep doing the same thing over and over.

A: Then we agree, a teacher does *have* to know something about learning theories to be able to teach *well!*

C: I didn't say that.

B: No, he didn't say that. Knowledge of learning theories isn't necessary for good teaching.

C: Right!

A: But it sure can help.

B: How?

Different Kinds of Learning?

A: I'm confused. I thought learning was all the same until I started thinking about it.

B: What do you mean?

A: Well, if I learn how to spell a word like "Mississippi" or learn a spelling rule like "i before e except after c," then I know something I didn't know before and I can spell or repeat and use the rule pretty automatically without thinking. That's one kind of learning.

B: It's the only kind, really. It's the kind of learning that goes on in school, isn't it? There isn't any other kind of learning.

A: But learning the multiplication table and how to read and write are all "automatic" things we learn in school and use in our lives without ever thinking about them. Surely we must want to get students to learn other sorts of things that they will think about or with.

B: I'm not sure there are any other sorts of things. Whatever is learned in school ought to be something that is usable in an automatic way, shouldn't it?

A: That may be true of addition or dental hygiene, but surely not of things like critical thinking or creative writing. Such things can't be "automatic." And what about history? History isn't just a bunch of facts like "Mississippi" and "i before e" learned and strung together. It's really understanding what and why things happened in the past and how the past is related to our present and future.

B: Isn't learning history like that dependent upon learning elementary things? Facts and events eventually get linked together to make complex understanding. That's how learning history happens.

A: I don't think so. I think I'm talking about a different kind of learning. It's more like learning literature. It's not so important that you learn the plots and characters as it is that you learn how to appreciate good literature and get a sense of the major contributions people have made to our literary heritage.

B: You're convincing me that there's some kind of difference, but I'm not very clear on just what it is. I'm not very clear either if the way we learn such things must be different from the way we learn "Mississippi" or "i before e." Could you make that a bit clearer?

A Starting Place for Learning

A: Let's start at the beginning. You have to admit that a newborn infant has at some point had absolutely no experience of the world—even if you count prenatal "experiences" once sense receptors are physiologically formed. A baby is literally a "blank slate" waiting to be "written on" by experience.

B: No doubt about it. At some point we've had no experience and then we begin to have some. Even though some still believe in reincarnation and the possibility of having experienced the world in a previous life, I just can't buy the "recall theory of things previously known." But why can't it be true, as Chomsky the linguist argues, that we're born with a "deep structure," a framework or basic structure for the grammatical forms that human languages take or else we never could learn a language so easily and early on in life no matter how much "experience" is written on our blank slate. Or perhaps we could argue like Kant that we must be born with certain basic categories built into our minds like time, space, and causation, and logical ideas like identity, negation, and contradiction or else we wouldn't have any way to start sorting out our experiences. In any case a baby needs to have some kind of "instrument" to write meaningfully on the blank slate—some "concepts" and logical ways to treat and capture experiences or experience would just be a continuous and undifferentiated thing.

C: You two seem to force an either-or upon us. Either there is nothing in our minds at birth and we learn everything about the world through our senses or we are born with basic categories and logical ideas that help us make sense of the world and so learn about it through our basic mental structures. I don't think either argument is correct. Human beings generate—that is, construct—"structures," categories, and reasoning forms in the process of their active interacting with the world because they have disequilibrating experiences as they grow and develop.

A: That sounds good, but I'm not sure I understand what you mean by learning being "construction" and how that differs from my view that all knowledge comes from experience.

B: And how does it differ from my view if we all seem to come up with the same basic categories and logical forms? Doesn't that demonstrate that they are universally inborn human traits?

Learning and Behavior Change

A: I think the behaviorist has the best definition of learning for teachers to use. Learning is a change of behavior. We learn to swim and can do something we couldn't do before. We learn Freudian theory and then we can talk intelligently about ego, id, and superego; we learn to be unselfish and so show concern for others. To talk about learning as getting something into the head isn't very useful especially to an educator. There is no way to look inside. But you can see behavior change.

B: All that may be true, but even though I learned chemistry in high school I don't go around calling salt "NaCl" or water "H_2O" or mixing things in test tubes or using litmus paper or a Bunsen burner. If you mean I did those sorts of things while I was learning chemistry, you're right, but I don't know how else I could have learned chemistry. In any case, I don't behave differently now even though I learned and still remember some chemistry. My behavior hasn't changed.

A: Well, how would you define learning? As a meaningful experience, I suppose?

B: Not exactly, but surely meaningfulness has to enter into it, doesn't it? Learning can't just be changing one's behavior whether it's meaningful to the individual or not. Let me grant that sometimes teachers do want to change their students' behavior, but you must grant me that sometimes teachers want students to understand things or appreciate things and that seems different to me.

A: It's not really different. When we say a student has learned and understood something, we mean if we ask him or her to explain it to us, then he or she could do it. That's producing "an explaining behavior" that the student couldn't do before.

B: That seems like an odd way to talk. Aren't you confusing evidence for learning, the explaining behavior, with learning itself as a "coming to understand something"? Couldn't I read a novel and understand it and appreciate the author's skillful writing without ever explaining or telling anybody anything about it? I'd probably not behave any differently either after reading it.

A: But if you were a teacher and your students read the novel, you'd have to have them do something like write an essay or answer some relevant questions before you could legitimately say they learned it.

B: That's what I mean. You're confusing evidence for learning with learning.

A: No, I'm not. If your students never behaved any differently after taking your literature course, like becoming poetry readers or play goers, say, then would you feel that they had learned anything worthwhile?

The Scientific Status of Gestalt and Behaviorist Theories

A: The most important thing about human learning is our mental grasping of meaning, of seeing things come together in a pattern as a whole.

B: I don't deny that in our personal experience of learning things, we might feel that way, but a scientific theory of learning can't be based on subjective, private feelings. It must be based on publicly observable behavior. That's important for teaching, too; teachers can't see inside a student's head, but they can see what students are able to do.

A: But such "seeings of patterns" or wholes are objectively demonstrable. Tell me what you see when you look at this.

xxoxxoxx

B: I see three pairs of x's separated by two o's.

A: And what do you see here?

ooxooxoo

B: Just the opposite, three pairs of o's separated by two x's.

A: Notice anything about the o's?

B: Yes, when I look closely at the second figure, the o's are not quite continuous circles. I didn't notice that at first.

A: What you do see now?

o ox o ox oo

B: I see five different units: two ox's, two o's, and one oo.

A: They really are the same letters as before though.

B: But with the spacing changed, they group differently! Why is that?

A: What you've just done is demonstrate publicly and objectively three Gestalt principles of human perception and learning. We human beings are "wired" to group, or see as a single unit, those things that are similar to one another, as in the first two figures pairing all x's or o's, and those things that are closer to one another, like the ox's in the last figure, even when they're not similar. We also seek the "best form" by ignoring discrepancies and so "close" the gaps in the o's in the second figure to make them what we think they were meant to be.

B: But you're still talking about what happens in the head, and while you give some objective evidence to support your theory, I still think that treating learning as a change in observable behavior that is brought about by some observable and manipulable reinforcer is a much more scientific and teacher-useful way to explain, predict, and control learning than it is to treat learning as an individual's organizing and patterning of experience.

A: But seeing a pattern, having things come together, and make sense is just what "reinforcing" is for human beings when they really learn something, isn't it? And using objective evidence to support our claims is what makes something scientific, not whether it's visible, invisible, in the external world, or in the head.

Which theory has the best claim to scientific status? To teacher usefulness?

Different Teaching-Learning Strategies

A: If you're ever going to learn to write well, you must first learn all the basics: sentence and paragraph structure, grammar, making transitions, making outlines, etc., and then all you need to do is put them all together.

B: That's easier said than done! Haven't you ever heard that the sum of the whole is greater than its parts? Writing isn't just mechanically putting things together to form a complex activity, it requires sensitivity to meaning and having a meaningful "message" to impart.

A: Sure, but you can't do that if you don't know the basics.

B: But you can know the so-called "basics" and still not write well.

A: OK, how would you try to get someone to learn to write well?

B: I'd get them to do a lot of writing that I'd supervise closely and whenever they wrote a good tight paragraph or a really well organized essay or a creative story and things like that, I'd give them positive reinforcement.

A: What's that got to do with "sensitivity to meaning and having a meaningful message to impart"? It sounds as though you would be telling them they did well and that their techniques were good, but you wouldn't be responding meaningfully to the messages they were sending.

B: I never thought of it that way. Maybe I could get them to approach each writing assignment as if it were a problem. People who solve their own problems find the outcome meaningful, don't they?

A: Yes, but writing isn't "problem solving" except if taken in a most strained sense of the term. And writing isn't creating meaning just for yourself either. It's trying to express yourself in communication with others. And for that you need the basics and there's no way to get the basics except to do them over and over.

B: But how do you get them to work altogether in a meaningful way?

A: It just happens, believe me.

What is at issue here? How do you "get it altogether"?

Teaching, Learning, and Stages of Development

A: The mind of the child is different from that of the adult. I don't mean that the child is just less informed and less practiced in thinking; I mean children literally do not think the same way as adults do.

B: Humbug! All minds young and old work the same way. All minds group things, perceive wholes, and see relationships. Children and primitives solve problems just as adults and scientists do: sometimes by trial and error and sometimes by insight and orderly hypothesis testing.

A: But children consistently make mistakes about certain kinds of relationships, like the conservation of volume findings that Piaget's clay sausage and water cylinder experiments point out. When they are older, they never make such mistakes.

C: Did you or Piaget ever try to correct their mistakes and teach them conservation? I've done it with six-year-olds using operant conditioning
and it gets results! They give the proper responses after only a few trials.

B: But did they understand conservation, I wonder? I agree with C about
one thing at least. Teaching can bring about *mental* transformations that
a theory like Piaget's relegates to development and age. I think we can
teach six-year-olds to conserve and even to be logical, which isn't supposed to happen until later.

A: That's impossible!

B: Then what are teachers supposed to do, sit around and wait until children's minds develop?

Learning to Read

It was time for reading in the first-grade class. The children always looked
forward to reading. They knew that reading was important and "grown-
up." So they were eager to learn.

The children already had learned the sounds associated with the individual letters of the alphabet. Today, the class would begin to put letters together to make words and would try to read these words. Their teacher
began with examples of some simple words: cat, bat, fat. The children repeated these after the teacher read them. After several examples, the
teacher wrote "mat," a word the children had not seen before, on the chalkboard and asked if anyone could read it. Immediately, a number of eager
hands shot into the air. One of the children read the word correctly. The
teacher and class applauded the effort. Again, the teacher wrote an unfa-
miliar word on the chalkboard. This time, the student who volunteered
didn't read the word correctly the first time, but did on the second attempt.
She was applauded, also. This process continued through many more examples until most of the children had responded. Some stumbled at first,
but with further examples, it became apparent that most of the children
were able to read the simple words the teacher gave. They were very
proud of themselves and wrote down the words on the board so that they
could take them home and read them to their parents.

If you were the teacher, how would you interpret what happened? Can
Gestalt theory explain this learning? What do you think Dewey would say
about this case? Can the learning be interpreted in terms of Plato's theory?
Can Locke's theory or behaviorist theory give insight into what occurred?
If you had to develop strategies to help children learn to read, what learning theory would be most helpful? Do you know any other approaches to
teaching reading? What learning theories do they seem to be based on?

Learning Facts and Structures

A: I don't know why I bother to work so hard to teach U.S. history. I just read that a sample of adults only ten years out of high school barely could answer 30 percent of a set of simple factual questions of the sort given in the seventh- and eighth-grade U.S. history tests.

B: It does make you wonder, doesn't it? I teach chemistry and while I'm sure no one forgot what H_2O is, H_2SO_4 and HNO_3 probably are meaningless symbols to my students a few years after they graduate.

A: I'm embarrassed to say they don't mean much to me either and I took chemistry to meet my undergraduate science requirement! I wouldn't dare ask you if you knew who won the election of 1848 or who was president on the eve of the Great Depression.

B: Thanks for not asking! Maybe it's not really important that students later on in life can't remember and replicate everything they learned in school.

A: But then why bother to teach them all those things? Why not just teach them the structure of the subject?

B: Because you can't get to really know history or chemistry without knowing basic facts, even though you can learn the basic facts in a subject without really coming to know the structure of the subject. But I'm confused now. You talk as if the structure of a subject is something apart from and different from the "facts" of a subject.

A: Well it is, isn't it? If you know the structure of a subject like chemistry, then you know that there are chemicals and chemical reactions of certain sorts. So when you read a newspaper article about the need for calcium in preventing bone deterioration in older people and explaining it in chemical terms, you don't recall any chemistry facts or formulas, you just use the structure you've learned to interpret and understand the article.

B: Do you mean you think people can forget all the facts of a subject and still know its structure?

A: Sure, why not?

B: And they don't ever need to be able to tell you what the structure is?

A: Right.

B: Wrong!

Learning Theory and Artificial Intelligence

A: The best model available to us today for developing a sound learning theory is the computer and artificial intelligence.

B: Haven't you got that the wrong way around? Don't we design computers and computer programs in certain ways because we think that's the way our minds must process information, calculate, think, and learn? The human mind and human learning are the models for artificial intelligence and computers—not the other way around!

C: No, you're both wrong. We design computer programs the way we do because of the basic constraints put on us by the kind of hardware we have and the programming languages we've invented to fit both the hardware and our programming purposes. Neither computers nor minds are models.

A: Wait a minute. I still think computers are a lot like human minds and brains. The hardware is like the brain; the software is part brain, part mind; and the actual data entered, produced, stored, retrieved, used, etc., is just like us doing all the "mental" things in our minds that humans do ... including learning!

Who is right: A, B, or C? Why?

Learning to Balance Chemical Equations

Mr. Johnson was teaching his chemistry class to balance simple chemical equations, for example, $MgCl_2 + NaBr \rightarrow$? Knowing how difficult this was for some students, he took an entire class period to do examples on the chalkboard and to answer questions about them. Then, he assigned a set of problems as homework.

The next day, Mr. Johnson found that many of his students had been unable to even begin the homework problems. They were completely lost. So Mr. Johnson tried to uncover the difficulty these students had.

Mr. J: Can someone explain what problems you had?

Abby: I took notes on what you did yesterday, Mr. Johnson. I understand that a reaction takes place and that the numbers of atoms must be the same on each side of the equation, but when I tried to do the problems, I just couldn't seem to get started.

Mr. J: Well, you have the basic ideas right. Who can tell us how to start this problem: $MgCl_2 + NaBr \rightarrow$.

Lee: I suppose the products should be written down.

Mr. J: Sure. What will the products be?

Connie: Well, the elements "switch" partners. So the products must be something like MgBr + NaCl.

Delilah: But that's not quite enough. You have to have the right formula for the compounds. You need to think about the valence numbers.

Mr. J: Good. What should the formulas be?

Elsie: Na is OK because Na is + 1 and Cl is – 1, that comes out to zero. But

Mg is + 2 and Br is   1, so 2 Br is needed to get a sum of zero. The formula should be $MgBr_2$.

Mr. J: All right. So now we have $MgCl_2 + NaBr \rightarrow MgBr_2 + NaCl$. What's the next step?

Juan: You have to check to see if equal numbers of atoms are on each side of the equation. There's one Mg on each side, so that's OK. Na is balanced too. Chlorine and bromine are unbalanced. On the left, there's one bromine and two chlorine atoms, but on the right there's one chlorine and two bromine.

Mr. J: How do we get those to be balanced?

Gerry: That's where I'm stuck. How do you do that?

Heath: You use coefficients. If we put a coefficient of 2 in front of NaBr, that gives us two of each of Na and Br on the left side and so the bromines are balanced.

Gerry: But then the sodiums are unbalanced. Is that supposed to happen?

Isaac: That's all right, because it can be balanced again. If we then put a 2 in front of NaCl on the right, everything comes out: $MgCl_2 + 2NaBr \rightarrow MgBr_2 + 2NaCl$. On each side, there are two sodium, two bromine, two chlorine, and one magnesium atom.

Gerry: Is there a formula for knowing how to do this?

Mr. J: The only formula I can give is looking carefully at the equation and doing some careful thinking. There's no standard procedure I can give you except to keep always in mind that you need to equalize and balance things. Just think about the things the class has mentioned. What I want you to do now is to rework the first homework problem. At least get something down on paper. That will give you a place to start. Then think and do *balancing*.

The students tried it. Some still had trouble, but when their thoughts were written down and their errors pinpointed, through their attempts to do the problem, they seemed to gain understanding of the balancing process. This procedure continued through the rest of the homework; the students did a problem and then the problem was discussed. By the end of the class, nearly everyone was able to do the problems

How do you account for the students' difficulties? Why do you think they could not do the work, even though several of them could at least verbalize the steps needed to do it and even though Mr. Johnson had carefully explained the process in the lesson the day before? Why were the students more successful the second day? Are there learning theories that would explain this success? How would a computer solve chemical equations? What would Vygotsky, and Lave and Wenger, say about this case— and especially about the classroom discussion Mr. Johnson conducted?

The Evaluation of Verbal and Skill Learning

A: How dumb! All the years I've been teaching I've treated student learning as if it referred to the things my students came to know and wrote down on their tests.

B: What's wrong with that?

A: Well, I assumed that anything they know can be put into words. So if I wanted to know if they've learned the sum of 2 + 2 or Einstein's theory, I'd ask an appropriate question and get back "4" or "E = mc²."

B: Of course.

A: But when I consider my own experience, I can't say anything very specific after I've learned things like how to juggle or how to add. It's not what I can say that counts; it's what I can do.

B: You're confusing me. What's wrong with saying if you learned something and still know it, you should be able to say it and write it down?

A: Nothing, if you'll accept as evidence that I learned how to juggle my saying that "I can keep three balls in the air at the same time."

B: I see what you mean. There's something funny going on here. Let's try to sort it out.

A: OK. If I say E = mc² in answer to a test question, at least you know I've learned the formula, but you don't really know if I understand it or if I've learned to use it.

B: Right, but I could ask you some more questions to see if you understand it and know how to use it.

A: Yes and no. Yes, more verbal exchange would help you judge whether I understood it, but to see if I know how to use it, you'd have to see me use it correctly and probably more than once.

B: So with things like E = mc², we can say what we've learned directly in words, but with things like juggling or using a formula, things we learn how to do, we can't *say* them, we can only *do* them and demonstrate our learning of them through action not words.

A: Right. Now how would you find out if the students in this school have learned scientific method, art appreciation, and good citizenship?

B: I'd give them standardized tests.

Learning the Meaning of Adding

Teacher: Today class, we're going to learn a new way to add.

Tom: We already know how to add. You'll confuse us.

Teacher: I don't think so. In fact, I believe you'll be better "adders" when we're done. What do you think the sum of 5 + 6 is?

Mary: Why it's 11, of course.

Teacher: Not this time. The answer to this problem is 14.

Li: How can that be?

Teacher: The sum is 14 because I was adding in the base 7 number system.

Mary: What does "base 7" mean?

Teacher: Remember how I explained that our number system is base 10? That means it's based upon groups of ten objects.

Tom: So base 7 means it's based upon groups of seven objects?

Teacher: Right! And so when we put 5 things and 6 things together in base 7, we can make 1 group of seven and have 4 left. Thus 14.

Li: I think I see. When we add 5 + 6 in base ten we get 11 because there's 1 group of ten and 1 left over.

Teacher: That's right!

Tom: Gee, I never knew that before.

Mary: So from 45 plus 26 we can make 7 groups of 10 plus 1, and that's why the sum is 71. 1 can really see how adding works now. I think it will be easier from now on!

Does the idea of learning the structure of a subject seem to be at work here? Before this lesson, did the students really know how to add? How do you explain the understanding they gained? Was the lesson a worthwhile one? Would any other learning theories shed light on this episode?

Learning Shakespeare

At Ridgemont High School there were two sections of senior English. The two instructors, Ms. Wilson and Mr. McGregor, taught basically the same material on the same schedule so that films, speakers, and other resources could be shared between the classes. In two weeks' time, they were beginning a unit on Shakespeare, and in the lounge one afternoon they were discussing the objectives they should have for their unit.

Mc: We probably should cover one tragedy, one comedy, and one history.

W: That sounds good. How about *King Lear, A Midsummer Night's Dream, and Richard III*—these are pretty representative?

Mc: Fine. What should the students be responsible for?

W: Just the basics, I suppose—major characters, the plots, some of the notable literary devices Shakespeare used.

Mc: Alright, but I'd like to do a little more besides.

W: Oh? Like what?

Mc: Just some background things. You know, like some of Shakespeare's biography, the times in which he wrote, the politics, the state of the theater. I want to help my students gain an appreciation for Shakespeare, to help them enjoy his works and read more of them.

W: That would be interesting to do, Bill, but isn't that getting off the track? After all, our purpose is to help the students learn Shakespeare's plays.

Mc: That's just my point. Learning Shakespeare's plays means more than knowing plots and characters. Learning Shakespeare's plays means knowing as much as you can about them and having an appreciation for them. If you don't have those things, you don't really know his plays.

W: I can't agree with you. For one thing, it's important for students to know the plots and characters of Shakespeare's plays. Those are what college boards and colleges expect them to know. And anyhow, how can you teach and test for appreciation? All we can do is teach the facts. There's no way teachers can convince students to appreciate something or find out if they really do.

Mc: I don't care what colleges want. I think appreciation can be taught. Maybe I can't convince students that they ought to appreciate Shakespeare by telling them they should, but I can show them how to bring together all the related aspects of Shakespeare's plays—their politics, humor, creativity, and so on. And I can encourage them to examine their feelings about Shakespeare. When I do all that, I think my students are bound to find Shakespeare's plays interesting and worthwhile.

W: I'm sorry but I can't buy that. Some students just don't like literature, period. And those who do will enjoy it regardless of what teachers do. No, I think we should stick to the basics and teach those well. That's what the students want and need, and that's all we have time for.

Mc: Well, Peg, I don't think we'll agree on this. I think your view of learning is too narrow. I think we can have students learn plots and characters and also really learn Shakespeare's plays in my broad sense. One follows from the other.

W: I wish you were right, Bill. You follow your plan; I'll follow mine. At the end of the unit, let's try to see who was closer to the truth. How *will* you test for appreciation?

Learning Responsibility

Ms. Epstein felt that a vital part of her social studies course should be devoted to the discussion and learning of social responsibility, that is, the obligations of the individual to others in society, and vice versa. To other teachers who thought that this sort of work should not be included, Ms. Epstein would say, "What is *social* studies, after all, if not the study of society, how people live together? Being responsible to one another is an important part of social living that must be learned."

So, along with the facts of history, politics, economics, and government, Ms. Epstein tried to get her students to think about such topics as trust, truth telling, promises, and benevolence whenever this was possible and appropriate.

One day, after beginning a lesson on some of the great American industrialists—Rockefeller, Carnegie, Vanderbilt, Guggenheim, and their philanthropy—Ms. Epstein brought up the subject of generosity. She asked if anyone would call these men generous?

The students' views were diverse. Helen thought that these men certainly were generous since they had given away so much money. Jack reminded the class that the fortunes had to come from somewhere. He argued that the men were not really generous because they had gotten their money from the sweat of others. It was the people's money to start with, he said, and they only gave a small part of it back. The argument went back and forth with much of the class participating. No conclusion was reached about Ms. Epstein's question except that it was a difficult and important question to think about.

Just before the end of class, Roger asked a question of Ms. Epstein. "Ms. Epstein, we've talked about social responsibility quite a bit. On our semester exam, will you give us questions about our knowledge of social responsibility?"

Ms. Epstein replied, "I think it's important for everyone to develop their own thoughts about that subject and to be able to communicate those thoughts effectively. But to be able to speak or write knowledgeably and thoughtfully about social responsibility does not mean that one has learned to be a socially responsible person. I'll know that you have learned that when I see you actually being responsible. Teachers don't need written exams to find out if their students have learned some things."

What do you think of Ms. Epstein's criterion for having learned to be socially responsible? Is she right? Could she test for it? Is it right, is it socially responsible to let the class discussion end without a conclusion and no answer to the question of generosity?

How might various learning theories be applied to the learning of social responsibility? Is the idea of learning social responsibility ambiguous? Are there other things we talk about teaching and learning that are similarly ambiguous?

Culture and Learning

A: Ever since we've had a sizeable group of people from the Pacific Islands settle in our town, I've had trouble teaching their children.

B: What kind of trouble?

A: Well, whenever I ask questions of the class, they never volunteer answers and even if I call on them directly, they hold back and seldom respond when I sense that they know the answers. It's frustrating, because "questioning and answering" is one of my key techniques for fostering learning!

C: I've noticed the same thing about these kids.

B: Me, too. Maybe their mastery of English is poor and they have difficulty understanding us?

A: No, their English seems fine to me. They don't seem to be having the difficulties the ESL students have. It's almost like they're afraid to answer me.

C: I'm trying to recall if this happens equally with boys and girls?

A: Come to think of it, it's mainly the boys who hold back.

C: Maybe in their culture males are not questioned by female authority figures. Maybe answering would lower their status, especially if they get the answer wrong!.

B: Or maybe they're just not used to this question-and-answer schema of teaching and they expect to be told about what is to be learned, not questioned about it.

A: I suppose that's possible, but is it really so hard, especially for young people, to rise above their cultural ways and adapt to our teaching-learning styles?

C: Perhaps it's not just a question of style. Maybe they perceive the situation in our classrooms as highly competitive and enhancing the value of the individual over the group, whereas in their culture the group counts for much more than the individual and it's almost immoral to pat yourself on the back.

A: Well, we seem to have a lot of "maybe's" here! How are we going to find out if any of them are true? And more importantly, how can we help these kids be learners in this new culture in which they find themselves? I think that as teachers we have a duty to use culturally sensitive teaching methods as much as possible. We can't just give new migrants lower grades because they don't adapt, can we?

B: I never thought of that. I guess I do grade the kids we have been discussing differently without realizing it.

Individualized Learning

Bob was a first-year teacher in a fifth-grade open-space classroom. Bob, like all the other teachers of his teaching team, had responsibility for one homogeneously grouped math class. The math program of the school was designed as follows: each student progressed through a series of worksheets; when one worksheet was finished correctly, the student went to the next. In this way, skill in addition, subtraction, multiplication, and other areas was to be learned at an individual's own pace. The idea was that the teacher could give individual attention to those children who needed it.

Bob thought that this system made sense. He liked that the program was so individualized. The students seemed to like the class, too. They were rewarded by the evidence of their progress and by the praise Bob gave when papers were completed.

Before long, though, Bob began to be uneasy about the direction his math class was taking. He felt that he was not really "teaching" his students. They were just doing worksheets on their own. He had thought he would be able to work one-on-one with the children. Instead, he found he spent almost no time with anyone. There was constantly a line of five or six children either waiting to ask questions or waiting to have papers checked. Bob felt that he could not afford to give as much time to each child as he would have liked since it would be unfair to keep all the others waiting. The children who finished papers were congratulated and sent on to the next worksheet. The students who had questions were told to try to work out an answer by themselves. They often would, but this usually took the form of three or four unsuccessful guesses before the correct answer was stumbled upon. Furthermore, Bob was so busy at his desk that he had difficulty being sure students were working and behaving as they should. Some students seemed to be progressing much too slowly. Bob was concerned that this was because he had not watched these pupils closely enough. In short, Bob came to see himself less as a teacher and more as a "paper pusher." Bob's worst fears seemed to be realized when one day he held an addition game. Bob chose problems that all the students should have known, since they came from worksheets all the students had completed. Contrary to Bob's expectations, many of his students were unable to do the problems he chose. It appeared that, indeed, many of Bob's students were not learning.

Do you see any problems in the school's math program? What learning theories would support it as a good program? What theories might not support it? Bob's students were completing their worksheets, but were they learning? Could you suggest any ways to improve Bob's situation? Does John Dewey have anything to offer here?

A Problem with Multiple Theories of Learning

A: Perhaps you can help me. I've been trying to make sense of something, but I can't quite do it.

B: Maybe! What are you trying to understand?

A: I've been taking a course on learning theories and I've tried to use them to throw light on how I learned to juggle last semester.

B: That should be easy. I took that learning theories course last year. What's the problem?

A: There are two problems really. First, some theories don't seem to work at all, but if they're valid theories they should explain all cases of learning, shouldn't they?

B: Well, perhaps ... which theories don't seem to work?

A: Plato's theory for one. I didn't "recall" how to juggle, did I?

B: How do you know you didn't? If you didn't have an inborn ability to juggle you never could have mastered it, right? I've tried to learn how and I can't. I just wasn't born with the physical coordination juggling requires. Plato's theory doesn't explain it all, but there must be something to the idea of learning as developing inborn capacities.

A: OK, but Lockean and Gestalt theories don't work, do they?

B: Why not? When you were learning to juggle didn't you break the process down to simple elements, practice them, and then try to combine them into more complex actions? Sounds pretty Lockean to me! And you must admit you were pretty much a blank slate with regard to juggling when you began.

A: It seems to me that Locke was writing about ideas not about how motor skills are learned. Besides, if I was a blank slate then how could I have an inborn capacity to juggle?

B: Well, Locke did stress that we have inborn ("pre-wired") capacities or powers, although he seems to have been focusing on mental powers. But let's try the Gestalt theory. Didn't you just keep on trying until it all came together in a rhythm, a pattern, a smooth-flowing continuous action as a whole? One minute you couldn't juggle and the next you could! That's Gestalt! It must have been a bit like learning to ride a bike!

A: Yes, it was kind of like that. But getting really good at it took lots and lots more practice. It wasn't instantaneous.

B: Ah, but when practice improved your performance, we could say you were learning to juggle *better*. Whereas at the point you first could juggle, that's when you *learned to juggle*. It was all at once, like a flash of insight, a Gestalt event.

A: OK, you've convinced me that I could use Lockean, Platonic, and Gestalt theory to explain my learning to juggle when I only thought I could do it with behavioral, problem-solving, Piagetian, and information-processing theories. But that gets me to my second problem. If all of these theories can explain the same phenomenon, how do we know which is right?

B: Whoever said theories need to be right or wrong?

A: Don't they?

Notes

Chapter 2: Classical Theories

1. Plato, *Meno*, trans. Benjamin Jowett (Indianapolis: Bobbs-Merrill, 1981), p. 36.
2. Plato, *The Republic*, trans. H. D. P. Lee (Harmondsworth, England: Penguin Books, 1955), p. 283.
3. J. Locke, *An Essay Concerning Human Understanding*, Everyman ed. (London: Dent, 1947), p. 65.
4. Ibid., p. 26.
5. J. Dewey, *Democracy and Education* (New York: Macmillan, 1958), p. 164.

Chapter 3: Behaviorism

1. J. B. Watson, "Psychology as the Behaviorist Views It," in Wayne Dennis, ed., *Readings in the History of Psychology* (New York: Appleton-Century-Crofts, 1948), p. 457.
2. J. B. Watson, *Behaviorism* (New York: W. W. Norton, 1930), pp. 38–39.
3. E. L. Thorndike, *Educational Psychology: The Psychology of Learning* (New York: Teachers College Press, 1913), p. 16.
4. B. F. Skinner, "Teaching Machines," in *Cumulative Record*, enlarged ed. (New York: Appleton-Century-Crofts, 1961), p. 164.
5. B. F. Skinner, *Science and Human Behavior* (New York: Macmillan, 1966), p. 66.
6. Ibid., p. 229.

Chapter 4: Problem Solving, Insight, and Activity

1. J. Dewey, *Democracy and Education* (New York: Macmillan, 1958), p. 317.
2. W. Köhler, *The Mentality of Apes* (Harmondsworth, England: Penguin Books, 1957), p. 113.
3. B. Russell, *An Outline of Philosophy* (London: Allen and Unwin, 1948), pp. 32–33.
4. J. Dewey, *Democracy and Education*, p. 393.
5. Ibid., pp. 186, 179.

Chapter 5: Piagetian Structures and Psychological Constructivism

1. J. Piaget, "Piaget's Theory," in P. Mussen, ed., *Carmichael's Manual of Child Psychology* (New York: John Wiley, 1970), p. 704.

2. J. Piaget, *Psychology of Intelligence* (Paterson, NJ: Littlefield, Adams, 1969), p. 9.

3. See, for an interesting series of examples, P. Bryant, *Perception and Understanding in Young Children* (New York: Basic Books, 1974).

4. In his more recent writings, von Glasersfeld grapples at some length with problems like these; see Ernst von Glasersfeld, *Radical Constructivism: A Way of Knowing and Learning* (London: Falmer Press, 1995).

5. Ernst von Glasersfeld, "Introduction," in E. von Glasersfeld, ed., *Radical Constructivism in Mathematics Education* (Dordrecht, The Netherlands: Kluwer, 1991), pp. xiv–xv.

6. von Glasersfeld, *Radical Constructivism: A Way of Knowing*, p. 177.

7. See the papers collected in K. Tobin, ed., *The Practice of Constructivism in Science Education* (Washington, DC: AAAS Press, 1993), especially chapter 8, Elizabeth Jakubowski, "Constructing Potential Learning Opportunities in Middle Grades Mathematics."

Chapter 6: Social Aspects of Learning

1. Clifford Geertz, *The Interpretation of Cultures* (New York: Basic Books, 1973), p. 52.

2. John Dewey, *Democracy and Education*, p. 3.

3. Ibid., p. 344.

4. Ibid., p. 188.

5. Ibid., p. 255.

6. Elizabeth Cohen, *Designing Groupwork*, 2nd ed. (New York: Teachers College Press, 1994).

7. Charles Dickens, *Oliver Twist* (London: Penguin Books, 1985), pp. 110–111.

8. L. S. Vygotsky, *Mind in Society* (Cambridge, MA: Harvard University Press, 1978), ed. and tr. by M. Cole, V. John-Steiner, S. Scribner, and E. Souberman, pp. 79–80.

9. A. Brown and L. French, "The Zone of Potential Development: Implications for Intelligence Testing in the Year 2000," *Intelligence, 3* (1979): 258–259.

10. This is stressed by Kieran Egan, *Getting It Wrong from the Beginning* (New Haven, CT: Yale University Press, 2002), pp. 68–77, 174–182.

11. L. Vygotsky, *Mind in Society*, pp. 79–80.

12. A. Bandura, *Social Learning Theory* (Englewood Cliffs, NJ: Prentice-Hall, 1970), p. 22.

13. James D. Watson, *The Double Helix* (London: Weidenfeld and Nicolson, 1968), pp. 200–201.

14. John Dewey, *Essays in Experimental Logic* (New York: Dover, n.d.), pp. 13–14.

15. Jean Lave and Etienne Wenger, *Situated Learning: Legitimate Peripheral Participation* (New York: Cambridge University Press, 1991), pp. 49–50.

16. A. L. Brown and J. C. Campione, "Guided Discovery in a Community of

Learners," in K. McGilly, ed., *Classroom Lessons: Integrating Cognitive Theory and Classroom Practice* (Cambridge, MA: MIT Press, 1994), pp. 229–270.

17. Clifford Geertz, *The Interpretation of Cultures,* chapter 2.

18. Shirley Brice Heath, *Ways with Words: Language, Life, and Work in Communities and Classrooms* (Cambridge, UK: Cambridge University Press, 1983).

19. The study was by J. Herndon, as described in Jean Lave, *Cognition in Practice* (New York: Cambridge University Press, 1988), p. 66.

20. Barbara Rogoff, *Apprenticeship in Thinking* (New York: Oxford University Press, 1990), p. 6.

Chapter 7: Cognitive Structures and Disciplinary Structures

1. D. Newman, P. Griffin, and M. Cole, *The Construction Zone: Working for Cognitive Change in School* (Cambridge: Cambridge University Press, 1989), p. 1.

2. D. Ausubel, J. Novak, and H. Hanesian, *Educational Psychology: A Cognitive View,* 2nd ed. (New York: Holt, Rinehart and Winston, 1978), pp. 170–171.

3. J. Eaton, C. Anderson, and E. Smith, "Student Preconceptions Interfere with Learning: Case Study of Fifth Grade Students" (Unpublished paper, Institute for Research on Teaching, Michigan State University, 1983).

4. D. Norman, "What Goes on in the Mind of the Learner," in W. McKeachie, ed., *Learning, Cognition, and College Teaching,* New Directions for Teaching and Learning, no. 2 (San Francisco: Jossey-Bass, 1980), p. 43.

5. J. Bruner, *The Process of Education* (New York: Vintage Books, 1963), pp. 7, 18.

6. J. J. Schwab, "Structure of the Disciplines: Meanings and Significances," in G. Ford and L. Pugno, eds., *The Structure of Knowledge and the Curriculum* (Chicago: Rand McNally, 1965), p. 12.

7. Ibid., p. 14.

8. P. H. Hirst, "Liberal Education and the Nature of Knowledge" in P. H. *Hirst, Knowledge and the Curriculum: A Collection of Philosophical Papers* (London: Routledge and Kegan Paul, 1974), p. 44. Quoted by permission of the author.

9. D. C. Phillips, "Perspectives on Structure of Knowledge," chapter 11 in D. C. Phillips, *Philosophy, Science, and Social Inquiry* (Oxford, England: Pergamon, 1987).

Chapter 8: The Cognitive Science Approach

1. R. Lachman, J. Lachman, and E. Butterfield, *Cognitive Psychology and Information Processing: An Introduction* (Hillsdale, NJ: Erlbaum, 1979), p. 99.

2. Richard Mayer, "Learners as Information Processors: Legacies and Limitations of Educational Psychology's Second Metaphor," *Educational Psychologist, 31,* nos. 3/4 (1996): 155.

3. W. McKeachie, in W. McKeachie, ed., *Learning, Cognition, and College Teaching,* p. 89.

4. D. Norman, in W. McKeachie, ed., *Learning, Cognition, and College Teaching,* p. 42.

5. See the discussion in H. Gardner, *The Mind's New Science* (New York: Basic Books, 1985), pp. 171–181. See also Merlin Donald, who remarks that many cognitive scientists and philosophers, rather than explaining consciousness, try to explain it away; *A Mind So Rare* (New York: W. W. Norton, 2001).

6. J. Searle, *The Rediscovery of the Mind* (Cambridge, MA: MIT/Bradford, 1992), p. 45.

7. S. Erlwanger, "Benny's Conception of Rules and Answers in IPI Mathematics" Journal of Children's Mathematical Behavior, 1, no. 2 (1973): 7–26.

8. J. Fodor, *The Language of Thought* (Cambridge, MA: Harvard University Press, 1979), p. 64.

Annotated Bibliography

Bransford, John D., Brown, Ann L., and Cocking, Rodney R., eds. *How People Learn: Brain, Mind, Experience, and School.* Commission on Behavioral and Social Sciences and Education, National Research Council. Washington, DC: National Academy Press, Expanded Edition, 2000.

> An authoritative compendium of research-based information about how experts differ from novice learners, about how learning occurs, on design of learning environments, and with detailed examples of effective teaching in several subject areas. Almost as valuable for the references as for the actual discussions.

Brophy, J. *Motivating Students to Learn.* Boston: McGraw-Hill, 1998.

> Brophy's book is packed with information, and this sometimes makes it slow-going for the reader. But as well as giving an overview of theories of motivation, he also gives a large number of helpful techniques for promoting motivation to learn in the classroom that will be appreciated by those who persist. Thus, chapter 7—"Stimulating Students' Motivation to Learn"—is a goldmine on a topic that, frankly, we do not spend enough time on in our book.

Bruner, Jerome. *The Process of Education.* Cambridge, MA: Harvard University Press, 1977.

> This is Bruner's report of the famous conference he chaired at Woods Hole that gave rise to the new science curricula of the 1960s. Bruner discusses his notion of structure of knowledge, readiness for learning, motivation, and related topics. A clear, lively, and short classic.

Byrnes, James P. *Cognitive Development and Learning in Instructional Contexts.* Boston: Allyn & Bacon, 1996.

> Besides being up-to-date, informed by much recent research, this clearly written book has the great virtue of pulling together in separate chapters what is known about learning (and the impact upon it of developmental factors) in important subject-matter areas—reading comprehension, writing, mathematics, science, and social studies. (Too often we forget that learners are not just learning, but are learning a particular body of content.)

Cain, M. J. *Fodor: Language, Mind and Philosophy.* Cambridge, UK: Polity, 2002.

> Not for everyone; this is a clear account, aimed at the philosophically inclined reader, of the work of the philosopher of mind Jerry Fodor. Noted for his development of the view that mind is not a singular unified entity but a series of "modules," Fodor also argues that the "common sense psychology" all of us use in daily life is compatible with the physicalist view that reality is entirely physical in its basic nature.

Case, Robbie, et al. *The Mind's Staircase: Exploring the Conceptual Underpinnings of Children's Thought and Knowledge.* Hillsdale, NJ: Lawrence Erlbaum, 1991.

> The major author was a leading neo-Piagetian, and here the attempt is made to

combine the view that during child-development major systemic changes occur, with insights from the view that mind is modular. Part 1 is a very useful overview.

Cleverley, John, and Phillips, D. C. *Visions of Childhood: Influential models from Locke to Spock.* New York: Teachers College Press, 1986.

Although oriented more toward theories of child development, this book contains discussions of many of the figures considered in the present volume, and its material forms a nice complement. There are chapters on "The Thinking Machine," "The Ages of Man," and "The Child and the Environment," among others.

Cohen, Elizabeth G. *Designing Groupwork: Strategies for the Heterogeneous Classroom, 2nd ed.* New York: Teachers College Press, 1994.

This is an easy-to-read blend of relevant theory and "how to do it" practical advice. It covers the role of groupwork in classrooms, preparing students to work cooperatively, and how to ensure all students take an active role. It also discusses the use of groups in bilingual and multi-ability classrooms.

Dewey, John. *The Child and the Curriculum, and The School and Society, joint ed.* Chicago: University of Chicago Press, Phoenix Books, 1969.

"The Child and Curriculum," really a long pamphlet rather than a book, is a classic and readable turn-of-the-century statement of Dewey's view of the teacher's role as "psychologizer" of subject-content. Vastly influential on teachers over the past century.

Donald, Merlin. *A Mind So Rare: The Evolution of Human Consciousness.* New York: W. W. Norton, 2001.

An extremely lively argument, with some great "one-liners," that consciousness cannot be explained away in terms of brain operations. The conscious mind interacts with cultural artifacts and symbol systems. A great read, full of interesting information.

Donaldson, Margaret. *Children's Minds.* New York: Norton, 1979.

Although steeped in Piaget's work, Donaldson is forced to reject some of its features. She believes Piaget underestimates the huge potential possessed by the rational powers of young children. Too often, learning in schools does not tap these powers, and children start to experience failure. Bruner has said that the implications of this book for education are enormous.

Egan, Kieran. *Getting It Wrong from the Beginning: Our Progressivist Inheritance from Herbert Spencer, John Dewey, and Jean Piaget.* New Haven, CT: Yale University Press, 2002.

Rejecting the received dogma that teaching should be based on insights from research and theory about the nature of the mind (it has no one nature), Egan presents a no-holds-barred attack on principles such as "learning should proceed from the simple to the complex" that he claims were passed from Spencer to the progressives. Even if wrong, this fascinating book forces the reader to examine deep assumptions!

Evans, Richard I. *B. F. Skinner: The Man and His Ideas.* New York: Dutton, 1968.

A dialogue between interviewer Evans and Skinner; they cover a great deal of ground, including some of Skinner's views on education. A readable way to get a feeling for Skinner the man.

Evans, Richard I. *Jean Piaget: The Man and His Ideas.* New York: Dutton, 1973.

A dialogue between interviewer Evans and Piaget; very readable, and a painless way of becoming acquainted with Piaget's views. (His own original writings make extremely difficult reading.)

Feldman, S. Shirley, and Elliott, Glen R., eds. *At the Threshold: The Developing Adolescent.* Cambridge, MA: Harvard University Press, 1990 (paperback edition 1993).

This volume brings together experts in various aspects of adolescence who contribute informative and readable chapters on such matters as the influence of "pubertal processes," sexuality, friendship and peer relations, stress, and the mass media. The chapter on "adolescent thinking" is especially pertinent to the topics we have discussed in the present book, but virtually all of the articles in this collection will be informative for those who have to help adolescents to learn.

Gage, N. L., and Berliner, David. *Educational Psychology.* Boston: Houghton Mifflin, 6th edition, 1998.

This physically taxing book (nearly 680 pages!) is written by two leading educational psychologists, stalwarts of the so-called invisible college for research on teaching, who are steeped in the research literature. An authoritative tome!

Gardner, Howard. *The Mind's New Science.* New York: Basic Books, 1985.

This readable but nevertheless authoritative book gives an account of the history of "the cognitive revolution." Drawing on philosophy, psychology, anthropology, linguistics, and work on artificial intelligence, Gardner traces the lines of development of modern cognitive psychology.

Lave, Jean. *Cognition in Practice: Mind, Mathematics and Culture in Everyday Life.* Cambridge, UK: Cambridge University Press, 1988.

An anthropologist doing what is termed as "outdoor psychology," Lave studies how "just plain folks" learn to use math effectively in their everyday activities in culturally relevant settings (as opposed to the often artificial setting of schools where they often fail).

Lave, Jean, and Wenger, Etienne. *Situated Learning: Legitimate Peripheral Participation.* Cambridge, UK: Cambridge University Press, 1991.

This book is quickly becoming something of a "cult" document. Its discussion of a variety of apprenticeships in diverse communities of practice is fascinating, and the terminology used by the authors is appearing more and more frequently in the literature. A good and important read.

Lippman, Matthew. *Natasha: Vygotskian Dialogues.* New York: Teachers College Press, 1996.

A very accessible rendering of the major educational ideas of Vygotsky, Dewey, Mead, and Davydov on learning as communal inquiry and meaning-making.

Minsky, Marvin. *The Society of Mind.* New York: Simon and Schuster, 1986.

Unusual in its format, with one-page entries, this book is packed with novel examples and helpful diagrams. Minsky (a pioneer in the field of cognitive science) describes his theory about how the mind works, including, of course, how it learns. Critics have labeled the book "provocative," "enlightening," "revolutionary."

Newman, Denis, Griffin, Peg, and Cole, Michael. *The Construction Zone: Working for Cognitive Change in School.* New York: Cambridge University Press, 1989.

In the words of the "blurb" on the back cover, "The 'construction zone' is the shared psychological space within which teachers construct environments for their students' intellectual development and students construct deeper understandings of the cultural heritage embodied in the curriculum." Full of detailed classroom examples, and with many insights drawn from Vygotsky.

Norman, Donald A. *Learning and Memory.* San Francisco: W. H. Freeman, 1982.

A wonderfully readable introduction to modern cognitive psychology, written by one of its leading researchers and with chapters on the stages of information processing, semantic networks, schemas, and so forth, all clearly explained and with good examples.

Phillips, D. C. "The Good, the Bad, and the Ugly: The Many Faces of Constructivism," *Educational Researcher,* 24, no. 7 (October 1995): 5–12.

This essay surveys the terrain covered by the large number of constructivist sects, and sets out to clarify the similarities and differences between them. However, it does not develop criticisms or evaluations in any detail.

Rogoff, Barbara. *Apprenticeship in Thinking: Cognitive Development in Social Context.* New York: Oxford University Press, 1990.

As stated in the Preface, "Children's cognitive development is an apprenticeship—it occurs through guided participation in social activity with companions who support and stretch children's understanding of and skill in using the tools of culture." An important book with great relevance for the organization of classroom learning.

Shulman, Lee. "Knowledge and Teaching: Foundations of the New Reform," *Harvard Educational Review,* 57, no. 1 (February 1987): 1–22.

A concise statement of Shulman's views on the "subject-matter knowledge for teaching" or "pedagogical content knowledge" that expert teachers build up over the years. Based on study of how novice teachers change as they become more experienced, Shulman's work has led to a renewal of interest in the "psychology of subject-matter," and it has become the basis for work done under sponsorship of the Carnegie Foundation on new forms of teacher assessment.

Skinner, B. F. *Walden Two.* New York: Macmillan, 1962.

A novel in which Skinner describes his "utopia," run on behaviorist principles. Critics have labeled it "brisk," "alluring," and "sinister." Certainly it stimulates thought about the role of education in society, the importance of early education, and the role of rewards and punishment in fostering learning and shaping behavior.

Tobin, Kenneth, ed. *The Practice of Constructivism in Science Education.* Washington, DC: AAAS Press, 1993.

This collection illustrates the range of positions that call themselves "constructivist," even within the one field of science education. Some contributions are theoretical, others focus more on classroom practice. Ernst von Glasersfeld provides a very readable set of answers to 42 questions about constructivism

Vygotsky, L. S. *Mind in Society.* Cambridge, MA: Harvard University Press, 1978.

A collection of important papers, mostly previously unavailable in the English-speaking world, of the Soviet psychologist who died prematurely in 1934. Vygotsky was a pioneer of the view that individual development and learning are influenced by communication with others in social settings. His theories are an important corrective to some of Piaget's ideas.

Wertsch, James V. *Vygotsky and the Social Formation of Mind.* Cambridge, MA: Harvard University Press, 1985.

For those who want to pursue Vygotsky's ideas in more depth, this is a valuable guide. The first chapter is an interesting account of his life and leading ideas; later chapters get more difficult but still remain clear.